ME, Inc.
ACHIEVING LIFETIME FINANCIAL WELLNESS

The Financial Education Institute of Canada

ME, Inc.
Copyright © 2011, by The **Financial Education** Institute of Canada Inc.

All rights reserved, including the right of reproduction in whole or in part in any form, except by a reviewer who wishes to quote brief passages in connection with a review written for inclusion in a magazine, newspaper or broadcast.

Printed and Bound in Canada
Copy Editor: Christopher Cartwright, Penny Butt
Design: Bold Graphic Communication Ltd.

Library and Archives Canada Cataloguing in Publication
Watters, Graydon G., 1943-
    Me, Inc. : achieving lifetime financial wellness / Graydon G. Watters.
    ISBN 978-0-9867696-1-0
    1. Finance, Persona–Canada.   2. Retirement income–Canada.
    3. Investments. I. Financial Education Institute of Canada II. Title.
    HG179.W3865 2010   332.024'01   C2010-907114-X

Disclaimer
The information contained herein has been obtained from sources which we believe reliable but we cannot guarantee its accuracy or completeness. This book is not and under no circumstances is to be construed as an offer to sell or the solicitation of an offer to buy any securities. This book is furnished on the basis and understanding that The Financial Education Institute of Canada Inc. is to be under no responsibility or liability whatsoever in respect thereof. The author/publisher would welcome any further information pertaining to errors or omissions in order to make corrections in subsequent editions.

Table of Contents

Foreword v

Section 1: Lifetime Wellness 1
Making a Living versus Making a Life 2
What is Lifetime Wellness? 7
Guiding Principles for Lifetime Wellness 9
Goals, Objectives, and a Plan of Action 12
What is Your Philosophy Regarding Time Management? 16

Section 2: Financial Wellness 19
What is Financial Wellness? 20
Cash and Debt Management 23
ME, Inc. – Adopt an Entrepreneurial Mindset 28
The Science of Wealth Accumulation 34
What is Your Risk Tolerance? 38
Asset Allocation Strategies 42
Employer Pension Plans 101 46
What is Your Wealth Accumulation Philosophy? 53

Section 3: Investment Management – The Basic Essentials 57
The Magic of Compound Interest 58
Impact of Interest Rates on Bond Prices 63
Risk versus Chance 65
Put the Power of Dividends to Work for You 69
How to Harness Inflation 75
How to Diversify Your Portfolio 79
Dollar Cost Averaging 84
The Two Market Forces You Need to Follow 90
What is the "Best" Investment? 93
Only Two Ways to Increase Your Real Wealth 98

**Section 4: Investment Management –
Intermediate Tools & Techniques** 103
Influences on Investment Returns 104
The Rule of 72 108
Inflation – The Real Story of Purchasing Power 112
Price Earnings Multiples 115
How to Rebalance Your Portfolio 119

Why Big Losses Demolish Portfolio Returns 124
Recovery from Market Losses 127
Dividend Reinvestment Plans.. 130
Buy and Hold Strategy 134
Market Timing Strategy... 137
Professional Money Management Styles 140

Section 5: Investment Management –
Advanced Tools & Techniques **145**
Canadian Income Taxes.. 146
Taxflation 151
Should I Pay Down My Mortgage,
Top Up My RRSP, or Start Up a TFSA?... 155
Make Market Sentiment Work for **ME, Inc**.................................. 158
Understand Behavioural Finance to Improve Performance............ 162
Investment Market Forces.. 165
Two Invaluable Concepts to Enhance Investment Returns 168
Investor Psychology.. 171
A Long-Term History of Market Cycles 174
Investment Market Cycles 179
The Efficient Frontier.. 183

Section 6: Retirement Wellness.. **187**
How Much Money Will You Need to Retire? 188
Freedom 55 – Myth or Reality?.. 194
The Two Legged Resources Stool 197
Living Expenses Decrease in Retirement 201
How to Determine Your Retirement Age Goal 205
What is a Sustainable Withdrawal Rate?.................................... 209

Section 7: Afterword **215**
Putting Your Blueprint into Action! 216

Appendix 1.. **219**
Investment Tips 220

Appendix 2.. **223**
Best/Worst Days by Percent Change and
Point Change DJIA 1901 to 2009 (March) 224

FOREWORD

Mortgage, credit card bills, job stress, taxes, unpredictable markets and an uncertain future…

Is it any wonder that Canadians spend millions on lottery tickets each year? After all, who wouldn't want to pay off the mortgage, eliminate debt, and never have to work another day in their life?

Of course, a lottery ticket is not an investment. And your financial security – especially when you stop working - can't be left to pure chance. There is another way…

Consider this book your winning ticket. It may take a little longer to see your jackpot, but we promise that the odds of winning are way, way better than any lottery out there!

You may already be dreaming about how to spend your winnings. Now is the time to start reading and making those dreams come true.

P.S. In case you do hold the lottery ticket that turns out to be the Grand Prize Winner, you'll want to know a little more about how to hang onto your new wealth, so keep reading this book!

SECTION 1
LIFETIME WELLNESS

Making a Living vs Making a Life

We are fortunate to live in a country endowed with natural resources and rich in opportunity for those of us who wish to indulge ourselves.

When we were young and about to leave the nest to venture out on our own, our parents often gave us wise advice such as, "two people could live cheaper than one." Wow! They must have been talking about really small people because most couples constantly experience having too much month at the end of the money. Have you ever had that affliction? And that is the dilemma most of us find ourselves in today – one paycheque just doesn't cut it any longer. So many people are driven by the pursuit of materialistic goals to acquire consumer products – no matter what the cost. And what a price they must pay for the so-called "good life" as promoted by the print and electronic media.

The traditional family unit, which consisted of a working Dad who was the breadwinner and a stay-at-home Mom whose career was to raise the children, is a rarity today because the purchasing power of money has decreased and many of us want more than we can afford on one income. We have chosen to moonlight at two or three jobs and many have become a two-income family. This most often is at the expense of our other values. As well, the structure for many family units has changed with same sex marriages and the role reversal of stay-at-home dads. And many more women are pursuing a career either for self-fulfillment or for the benefit of their family or both.

Add to this mix the need to be a caregiver for an ageing parent. We find many families attempting to juggle too many needs – children, career, eldercare, personal health, and maintaining one's home; we realize that something has to give! One out of every four employees over age 40 is involved in care giving to an older person for over 30 hours per month. And any reasonable expectation would suggest that both the number of caregivers and the hours of care giving will only increase over time.

That is the dilemma most of us find ourselves in – one paycheque just doesn't cut it any longer.

It has often been said that parents are the ultimate circus performers who must create a daily juggling act of balancing their work, home, family, relationships, health, and financial concerns. The question that needs to be answered is, "How do you handle the work and non-work aspects of your life and still maintain your sanity?" The answer begins with life planning!

The Six Powers of Success™
In the course of our business affairs The Financial Education Institute of Canada offers workshops that emphasize setting goals that require a balanced approach to successful lifetime financial wellness. We utilize a knowledge tool that embraces a philosophy we call **The Six Powers of Success™,** which includes the following major components:

- Physical Health
- Precious Relationships
- Personal Control
- Profession/Career/Vocation
- Personal Fulfillment
- Pursuit of Financial Freedom

Take a moment right now to think about which three of **The Six Powers of Success™** are of greatest importance to you.

1. _____
2. _____
3. _____

You might be interested to learn how tens of thousands of participants have answered this question over the last three decades.

Lifestyle Importance at Various Ages

20 to 40	41 to 60	61+ 1980–1990s	61+ 2000s–2010s
Money	Health	Relationships	Relationships
Health	Money	Health	Health
Relationships	Relationships	Money	Personal Fulfillment

The Institute has observed the following results over the years:

- Younger Canadians almost always choose money first.
- Canadians in the second half of their careers are generally more established. They realize that in their fifties their physical bodies start breaking down and no amount of money in the world can buy back their health. For them, health becomes the number one power of importance.
- For most Canadians entering retirement, the number one focus shifts to relationships when they have more time to enjoy family and friends.
- Note how money declines in importance as Canadians age throughout their life cycle.

Several years ago the Institute observed a new trend with individuals nearing retirement (usually in their late fifties or early sixties) that money was no longer one of their top three choices; personal fulfillment had taken its place. Personal fulfillment includes things like: hearth and home, meaningful activities, spiritual inquiry/religion, volunteer/service, intellectual satisfaction, leaving a legacy, and so on.

The reasons why money declines in importance for older Canadians are threefold:

1. **Mortgage free** – homes paid off
2. **Empty nest** – children leave home
3. **Pension plans** – many years of employer and personal pension plan accumulation are coming to fruition.*

Canadians nearing retirement realize that these plans along with their government income security programs will provide an income replacement ratio that will enable them to have a comfortable lifestyle in retirement.

*Note: All of the participants in the Institute's surveys have the benefit of a company sponsored pension plan. We suspect the results with respect to the importance of money would be greater, (perhaps the number one concern) for employees that don't have a company sponsored pension plan.

Ten Secrets of an Anti-Aging Stress Reduced Lifestyle

1. Make a career or job you love
2. Share your dreams, goals, and values with your life partner or "best friend"
3. Acquire wealth and independence
4. Enjoy frequent vacations
5. Hire a personal coach and/or fitness trainer
6. Eat, drink, and be merry in moderation
7. Get lots of rest, relaxation, and 8-hours of sleep
8. Embrace life-long learning and share your wisdom
9. Cherish your relationships
10. Develop your spirituality and mission to others

Did You Know?

Holistic Approach

During one's career the three greatest powers usually consist of blending money, health, and relationships into a pyramid of success – a holistic approach to obtaining contentment, happiness, and self-satisfaction in one's life.

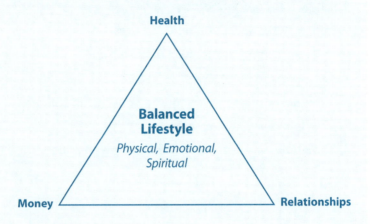

What is Success?

To laugh often and love much;
To appreciate beauty;
To find the best in others;
To give of oneself;
To leave the world a bit better, whether by a healthy child, a garden path, or a redeemed social condition;
To know even one life has breathed easier because you have lived;
This is to have succeeded!

– Ralph Waldo Emerson

What is Lifetime Wellness?

Lifetime Wellness is an ongoing process of creating goals and setting objectives at every stage of the life cycle – it is about living a happier, healthier life today while designing our life plans for tomorrow. Perhaps the greatest transition in our lives is the one we refer to as retirement. Successful financial and retirement plans are always a by-product of the development of a meaningful life plan. Life goals are generally focused on trying to balance one's work, family, and personal needs. However, the obstacles you must overcome in order to balance your goals, priorities, attitudes, and time for a happier more fulfilling and more productive life can be overwhelming.

For so many Canadians work is simply a means to an end. Many people live for today, conquering today's tasks, not planning for retirement. Some use today's financial rewards to provide for a secure retirement. What often gets lost in this scenario is all of the other aspects of living one's life.

In our constant pursuit of happiness, we first must learn the lesson that we don't become happy by pursuing happiness. We become happy by living a life that means something. Therefore, life planning is a conscious choice we make to design life goals; to create the lifestyle pursuit of our dreams; to self-actualize; in other words, to have it all.

> **Successful financial and retirement plans are always a by-product of the development of a meaningful life plan.**

The Scorecard We Call Life

Have you given serious thought and contemplation about what really matters on the scorecard we call life? Many of us seek out productive lives with high achievements; and some of us measure success by what we earn monetarily or by what stature we attain in our lives: presidents, chief executive officers, politicians, sports celebrities, actors, and other roads to fame.

While there is nothing wrong with this approach to life, all too often these goals are pursued to the exclusion of fulfilling relationships that are of even greater importance.

Many years ago we came across the following quotation that seems to say it all.

"The legacy of our lives is written in the hearts of those that love us."

Did You Know?

It's Not Just About the Money

Individuals who have had the greatest life successes most often share one common characteristic — a positive mental attitude!

Individuals who seem the happiest and most successful are most often those who have concrete goals and have implemented an action plan; and they always consider the glass to be half full.

Consider This!

Successful individuals tell us that goals as destinations matter less than the process itself; that getting there was most of the fun. When the ultimate goal becomes the process, the journey becomes the destination.

Don't count the days, make the days count.
— Muhammad Ali

To travel hopefully is a better thing than to arrive.
— Robert Louis Stevenson

Guiding Principles for Lifetime Wellness

Money permeates our lives throughout every aspect of the life cycle. Healthy attitudes with respect to money can enhance our lives; however a pessimistic or defeatist attitude can lead to money woes. At the other extreme some people will make money their god and in the final analysis it can just as easily destroy their lives.

We know that money can't buy happiness but we also know that it can make our life's journey much easier once we take control of our financial wellness.

Many people procrastinate retirement planning until the latter stages of their working careers. While it's better late than never, the earlier you start planning for retirement the greater your rewards. The following chart provides guidelines for three major stages of the life cycle.

Healthy Habits for Lifetime Wellness

Description	Early Adulthood Ages 21 – 40	Middle Adulthood Ages 41 – 60	Maturity Ages 61+
Cash Management	• Pay yourself first • Establish a budget • Build up cash reserve emergency funds • Pay off all debts • Establish a credit history	• Cash flow is your life blood • Focus on building net worth • Eliminate all debts prior to retirement	• Create a post-retirement budget
Home Ownership	• Save for first home purchase • Consider RRSP Home Buyer's Plan • Purchase home • Maximize mortgage payments and shorten amortization term	• Prior to retirement, pay off mortgage or downsize home	• Purchase home with an income potential i.e., duplex, triplex, or basement apartment • Sell home to obtain equity for investment • Consider lifestyle retirement community • Consider reverse mortgage only after all other options are exhausted

Description	Early Adulthood Ages 21 – 40	Middle Adulthood Ages 41 – 60	Maturity Ages 61+
Employer-Sponsored Pension Plan	• Take advantage of corporate capital accumulation plans and GRSPs if available • Maximize contributions to thrift or savings plans offered by your employer	• Obtain corporate pension projections every few years to ascertain retirement income • Learn about early retirement options • Research government programs – CPP/QPP and OAS benefits	• Establish income stream from corporate pension • Choose survivor options • Pension Income Splitting with spouse up to 50% before age 65
Investment Management	• Create an investment portfolio • Establish asset allocation strategies based on your risk tolerance and timeframes • Utilize dividend tax credit	• Create a portfolio for your financial independence • Maximize tax efficiencies with capital gains • Invest any inheritance received	• Reduce risk levels and create retirement income for at least six years forward • Maintain core long-term portfolio in growth assets with seven or more years timeframe to protect purchasing power
Risk Management	• Purchase insurance: property, life, and disability	• Consider critical illness, long-term care insurance	• Consider Universal Life insurance for tax effectiveness and estate planning

Tax Planning – Registered Investments	• Establish an RRSP for:
	  – tax reduction
	  – tax free compounding
	  – tax deferral
	• Establish an RESP for your children's education (if applicable)
	• Set up a Tax-Free Savings Account (TFSA)
		• Spousal RRSP (if applicable)
		• Open a self-directed RRSP plan (if feasible)
		• Maximize contributions to both RRSPs and TFSAs
		• Consider Tax Shelters
			• Top-up any unused RRSP contribution room
			• Convert RRSP to RRIF or Annuity or combination of both
			• Pension Income Splitting with spouse up to 50% after age 65

Estate Planning	• Create a relationship contract, cohabitation contract, or prenuptial agreement prior to marriage or living common-law • Establish a Will, Power of Attorney, and guardianship of children (if applicable)	• Review your Will periodically and at major life transition points e.g., marriage, divorce, birth of child, and so on • Create a living Will or medical directive • Set up family trust or informal trusts for children	• Create an estate plan and establish trusts and gifting for family members • Consider setting up TFSAs for your adult children • Business Succession Plans • Legacy Plans • Create charitable giving strategies
Life Events	These events can occur at any stage of the lifecycle. They can involve spouse and children (if applicable) and immediate and extended family members and may often require professional counselling and specialty planning through each life event transition: marriage, separation, divorce, birth, death, widow/widower, disability, disengagement, new careers, time management, relocation, empty nest, eldercare, and other wellness transitions.		

Did You Know?

Five Money Truths

1. Making money is a skill.
2. Keeping money is a discipline.
3. Spending money can become addictive.
4. What you spend money on identifies your values.
5. Managing money well is an art.

While it's better late than never, the earlier you start planning for retirement the greater your rewards.

Consider This!

If a person has a job he or she likes, with a reasonable standard of living, and has a disciplined retirement accumulation plan that will supplement Canada's Income Security programs (OAS & CPP/QPP), then that person already has financial independence.

The primary goal of all working Canadians is a worry free financially secure retirement.

The secondary goal is to leave an estate for loved ones or a legacy for community.

– *The Financial Education Institute of Canada*

Goals, Objectives, and a Plan of Action

Life is an ongoing process of creating agreements with oneself. Over the years you have learned that establishing goals, setting objectives, and creating an action plan are the keys to success. To achieve a goal you must have a clear-cut, focused disciplined approach to realize the goal. And it is important to state each goal specifically, to visualize the end result, to set a date for its completion, and to put it in writing.

Goals translate our visions into reality. Unlike wishes, which include dreams, fantasies, or products of wishful thinking, goals are more concrete and specific. In fact, the very foundation of your success has been and always will be your ability to create well-defined goals throughout your life. Let's take a look at some sample goals in the chart below. This is a template that you can use to create goals as the President for **ME, Inc.**

Sample Goal	Cost to Achieve	Completion Date	Steps to Complete
Short Term Goal *(Under 1 Year)* Join a gym to achieve better fitness and to lose 24 lbs.	$900 annual membership	M/D/Y	1. Sign Agreement for 1 Year term with gym at $75/month 2. Commit to go to the gym a minimum of 3 times per week
ME, Inc. Goal *(Under 1 Year)* _____ _____ _____ _____ _____	_____	M/D/Y	_____ _____ _____ _____ _____

Section 1 Lifetime Wellness

Sample Goal	Cost to Achieve	Completion Date	Steps to Complete
Medium Term Goal *(2 to 10 Years)* Catch up on unused RRSP contributions	$20,000 plus new Investments	50% by M/D/Y 50% by M/D/Y	1. Lump-sum deposit $5,000 2. Payroll plan $250/month 3. Tax refund from RRSPs – $2,000/year
ME, Inc. Goal *(2 to 10 Years)* _____ _____ _____ _____	_____	M/D/Y	_____ _____ _____ _____
Long Term Goal *(10 Years +)* Mortgage payout in 10 years.	$120,000 balance	M/D/Y	1. Annual lump sum of $4,000 2. Increase payment on renewal 3. Negotiate interest rate on renewal date _____
ME, Inc. Goal *(10 Years +)* _____ _____ _____ _____	_____	M/D/Y	_____ _____ _____ _____

Financial Goals are only "dreams" until they are visualized, articulated, time-bounded, and finally written down. Only then can a realistic plan be created to achieve your goals.

The process of setting objectives and creating a plan of action requires you to buy in with true commitment. There is no room for procrastination, especially when it affects your earning power from your career or from your investments. A person is what he or she believes.

Goals translate our visions into reality.

The goals you set always happen when you really believe in them and it is your belief in them that makes them happen. You are in control of your destiny and only you can make the decisions that affect your life and your finances. You are where the buck stops and the dollar begins. In the course of our lives we come up against many obstacles when even the best laid plans and goals are interrupted or run off course. The Great Recession of 2008–2009 decimated the financial and retirement portfolios of many investors. For those investors close to retirement it was particularly painful to watch their pension assets and investment portfolios go through such devastating declines in value.

For those of us here at the Institute, our goal is to help you restructure, re-build, and replenish your capital accumulation goals. By re-evaluating tried and true processes that have worked for investors throughout numerous cycles in times past it is our desire to provide you with the knowledge and tools required to reinvigorate life into your financial goals.

Formula for a Plan to Succeed
- Dare to Dream
- Formalize Goals
- Establish Priorities
- Set **S.M.A.R.T.** Objectives:
    - **S**pecific goal (seven words or less)
    - **M**easurable plan of action
    - **A**ttainable (goal must be achievable)
    - **R**ealistic with desired result
    - **T**ime-bounded (years to completion)
- Formalized financial goals for your retirement future are critical to your success.

Consider This!

The three greatest ways to build wealth are: *patience, patience, patience!*

Time will surely build wealth for disciplined, focused, patient investors.

Always remember that higher returns can only be obtained by assuming the risk of higher volatility. However, successful investors know that the returns are permanent while the volatility is temporary.

To think is easy, to act is difficult, to act as one thinks is the most difficult of all.
– Johann Wolfgang Van Goethe

Personal commitment is critical to the success of any plan. Without commitment, the goals of the plan are not likely to be met.
– Unknown

When you live by the crystal ball in making market forecasts you will always end up learning how to eat lots of broken glass.
– The Financial Education Institute of Canada

What is Your Philosophy Regarding Time Management?

Most of us understand the concept of time with respect to our investments and their various compounded returns. But what about the concept of time itself.

Imagine a person age 45 today, with an additional life expectancy of 40 years to age 85.

How long is each year? Most of us would respond with numerical data such as 12 months, 52 weeks, or 365 days. However, the response we're really looking for is how long does each year feel? Well, that depends on what kind of year you're having. If you're having a good year, time just flies; if you're having a bad year, time can never seem to move much slower.

How Much Time Do You Have Left?
(Assume Current Age to Life Expectancy of Age 85)

Description	Current Age				My Age
	25	35	45	55	
	TimeFrame to Age 85				
Number of Years	60	50	40	30	
Number of Seasons	240	200	160	120	
Number of Weeks	3,120	2,600	2,080	1,560	

Suppose we were to divide the next 40 years into weeks.
Well 40 years x 52 weeks = 2,080.
Now ask yourself, "How long does one week last?"
Not very long, in fact, a week can pass with the snap of your fingers.

Think about how quickly a week disappears – 2,080 after this week, 2,079 after the following week, 2,078 after the next, and after one year passes just 2,028 weeks would be left. When we measure our lives in terms of weeks, we realize that time is our best friend, the most precious ally we have, not just with respect to our investments, but to every aspect of our daily lives.

Count Your Blessings!
- Strive for balance in your life – **Heart – Body – Mind – Soul**
- Awake to each new day and give thanks for all that you do have
- Every day, every minute, every breath, truly is a gift
- Time is your greatest ally; it is the best friend you'll ever have

Time Management and Your Finances
Time presents us with our greatest opportunities; a resource that provides us with 86,400 seconds every day. And any of that time not put to good purpose is lost forever.

In matters of personal finance, procrastination reveals its true character – self-sabotage. The longer one waits to put money to work, the more money one will require when one eventually starts to save and invest. Retirement income is seldom a concern when we are young.

A house, a car, perhaps a boat or cottage, and travel, are higher priority items at that time in our lives. Too often, people reach age 55 or 60 and realize they have not adequately planned to meet their future expenses. That realization is frightening and, in most cases, will prevent them from acquiring the necessary capital for their retirement with financial security.

Make time work for you! Look at it as something under your control, something tangible. Time is your greatest ally.

> **In matters of personal finance, procrastination reveals its true character – self-sabotage.**

You have the opportunity to change the direction of your financial life and to develop meaningful interests for your retirement years. The process doesn't begin tomorrow. It begins now!

Consider This!

Work-Life Balance Top Concern for Workers

- Finding time for family outweighs fear of layoffs for today's professionals
- Of workers polled, 32% said the ability to balance business with personal and family demands was their number one priority
- Job security (22%) and competitive salary (18%) were the next two priorities according to Office Team – staffing services

Life for most of us it passes – day by day:
Sometimes in pain,
All too rarely with joy,
But mostly it just passes.
Until one day
Our precarious hold slips, is joggled,
And oh-so-nearly falls from our grasp.

Then we know, if it's not too late,
That each new day is too precious
Just to let pass.
It is instead a fresh gift given,
To be savored, whether in pain or with joy,
But always to be lived and somehow
To be given back again to whence it came.

– Larry Glover
A Momentary Candle

SECTION 2
FINANCIAL WELLNESS

What is Financial Wellness?

Financial wellness for **ME, Inc.** is the process of meeting your life goals through proper management of your finances. In simple terms, financial management is the process of gathering, understanding, implementing, and controlling your financial resources in order to use them more effectively now and in the future. Financial management is necessary if you wish to satisfy your own and your family's needs throughout your life cycle.

During your working years the focus on financial management is on wealth creation, accumulation, and conservation of assets. At retirement, your focus will shift to conservation and the distribution of your estate.

Setting the Stage
- What will it take for you to survive financially in the 21st Century?
- What strategies would you have to put in place to ensure that you will achieve financial and career success?
- What would it take to increase your career, relationship, and financial success and achieve a balanced lifestyle?

> **Financial wellness for ME, Inc. is the process of meeting your life goals through proper management of your finances.**

Two major shifts have occurred since the previous generation approached retirement:

- We are living longer, healthier lives, adding one to two years to our life cycle every decade.
- We are retiring earlier, often in our late 50s to early 60s.

Just as a chief financial officer develops plans to build a company, starting with a very solid financial foundation, so should **ME, Inc.** financial plans be carefully constructed – planning each step along the way.

Theory versus Reality
When it comes to financial management, historically the theory has been usurped by the reality.

In theory planning for financial independence should begin the day we enter the workforce.

The reality is that most individuals postpone their financial management to the latter stages of their working careers – they simply procrastinate.

So what is the ultimate goal of personal financial wellness?
Answer: To be financially independent; to have enough wealth to provide for your financial security. Fortunately, as the Chief Financial Officer (CFO) of **ME, Inc.** and the fact that you are reading this book, you have decided to take a proactive approach to secure your financial destiny.

Did You Know?

Attaining your financial goals requires a powerful and flexible financial plan. But a financial plan does not spring into existence by itself. It begins with your effort, your resolve, your honesty, and a few winces along the way.

Your financial plan results from the process of gathering, understanding, and managing your financial resources in order to use them more effectively to achieve your objectives. You don't get what you deserve — you get what you plan for!

Consider This!

The three most important questions most individuals want answered are:

- Will I have enough money to retire?
- At what age can I retire?
- How much do I need to save and invest to meet my objectives?

Life's arithmetic used to be much simpler — 1 career, 1 house, 1 marriage, 1 community, 1 crop of kids. What's your frenzy factor?

– Faith Popcorn

Many individuals are waiting for their ship to come in, but the sad truth is unfortunately 80% of them are sitting on a bench at the bus depot.

– Unknown

Cash and Debt Management

The best way to approach financial wellness is to think of you as the sole proprietor of a business called **ME, Inc.** Within **ME, Inc.** your primary position and title is President. However, when it comes to matters of finance you have other responsibilities to fulfill as the chief financial officer (CFO) for **ME, Inc.**

A business is typically formed to provide goods and or services to consumers with a goal of earning profits that increase the wealth of its owners. Similarly, the primary fundamental goal of every individual is to attain a worry free financially secure future. The goal of The Financial Education Institute of Canada is to provide you with all of the financial resources and knowledge tools you will need to achieve success within the pages that follow.

The first and most important rule of cash management is to **"pay yourself first."** Determine how much you can set aside to:

1. pay down debt
2. save and invest

Generally, it makes the most sense to eliminate any personal or credit card debt before embarking on a savings and investment program.

Most people look at their expenses and find nothing left for savings. You may be like these people – you don't have a structured plan for saving. The reason you don't is because you don't include yourself as one of your expenses! If you want to start saving wisely it will mean looking at your personal budget in a new way.

Your budget includes four major costs: housing, food, transportation, and personal items. Beyond these four costs you have all of your other monthly bills. Now add yourself to the list. Learn to develop a healthy selfishness about your money by placing you and your family first. Note that most budget (cash flow) calculators are designed to input your net income (gross income less payroll deductions and taxes) as the starting point, which would be your net income prior to calculating all of your other expenses.

ME, Inc. | Achieving Lifetime Financial Wellness

Cash and Debt Management for **ME, Inc.**

Old Way Monthly Budget	
1 Housing	$_____
2 Food	$_____
3 Transportation	$_____
4 Personal Items	$_____
5 All Other Bills	$_____
6 **YOUR SAVINGS**	$_____
Total Expenses	**$**_____

New Way Cash Management	
1 YOUR SAVINGS	$_____
2 Housing	$_____
3 Food	$_____
4 Transportation	$_____
5 Personal Items	$_____
6 All Other Bills	$_____
Total Expenses	**$**_____

Bring your regular savings plan to the top of the list and determine the amount you can save each month whether it's 4%, 7%, or 10% of your gross income. Put a figure in at the very top of the list for savings and then you can look after your housing, food, transportation, personal care and remaining bills. "Pay yourself first" is the most important premise in beginning a savings plan.

Section 2 Financial Wellness

Pay Yourself First – 10% Guideline

Are you aware that for most Canadians their largest expenses are deducted at source from their paycheque – government taxes, Canada/Quebec Pension Plan (CPP/QPP), Employment Insurance (EI), often as much as 35% or more of their hard earned dollars?

The secret to acquiring a nest egg for your future is to pay yourself first. We recommend saving 10% of your gross income throughout your working years, to ensure adequate assets are accumulated for your retirement. When you invest in a company pension plan or a RRSP you legally defer paying taxes on the capital invested until the monies are removed, ideally in the distribution phase of your life at retirement.

One further note – dependent on whatever your employer's pension plan requires you to contribute; invest the balance in your personal RRSP, TFSA, or other non-registered investments to make up the 10% guideline. For example, if your employer plan requires a 6% employee contribution, then allocate the remaining 4% from your gross income to your personal plans.

The primary payment during your working career is to develop the discipline of paying yourself first to ensure adequate financial reserves for your retirement.

Did you know that the wealthy always have the habit of paying themselves first; and the poor always pay themselves last?

Your key goal by the time you reach retirement is to have a plan that continues to pay yourself first. Ideally, you will have created a substantial cash flow to maintain your lifestyle from the savings you have diligently accumulated over the years in your government pensions, employer pensions, and personal pensions (RRSPs) and non-registered investments.

Helpful Hints for Successful Budgeting

- Determine exactly how much an item will cost and what sacrifices will have to be made in order to make your goals a reality.

- Make sure your budget is flexible rather than precise. Allow for a degree of error. Don't strap yourself to the point where you lose interest in your original goal.

- Allow for the unexpected in your plans. Situations change and emergencies come up. Don't allow these happenings to cause you to lose sight of your original goal.

- Make sure the budget is compatible with your personality and habits. No one knows you better than you know yourself. So plan accordingly, in line with your strengths and weaknesses.

- You have to know where your money is going, so you must develop a record keeping system that is easy to follow. It is helpful to break down your expenses into: fixed, variable, and discretionary – as well as short-term and long-term expenses.

- Beware of buying things on impulse and do not buy on credit.

- Keep your borrowing to a minimum and, if you do need to borrow, find the cheapest source of credit available.

- Be sure to have a monthly and an annual "financial fire drill" to compare your actual experience with your budget objectives:

    - What parts of my budget are working well?
    - What do I need to change?
    - How can I improve the return on my savings?

Consider This!

Successful individuals tell us that goals as destinations matter less than the process itself; that getting there was most of the fun. When the ultimate goal becomes the process, the journey becomes the destination.

I have enough money to last me the rest of my life, unless I buy something.

– Jackie Mason

A penny saved is a penny earned.

– Benjamin Franklin

Today there are three kinds of people; the haves, the have-nots, and the have-not-paid-for-what-they-haves.

– Earl Wilson

ME, Inc.
Adopt an Entrepreneurial Mindset

The chief financial officer (CFO) of a company is assigned with the responsibility of managing the financial affairs of the company to ensure its success. Therefore your first order of business as the CFO of **ME, Inc.** is to conduct an honest assessment of your current finances. That will entail drawing up a personal balance sheet to provide a rough estimate of your assets and liabilities. In simple terms, list everything you own that is sellable (assets) and subtract everything you owe (liabilities) to determine your net worth. Ideally your assets are greater than your liabilities, and if not, your next order of business will be to focus on debt elimination. Use Sample Inc. in the following table as a guideline to complete your personal balance sheet for **ME, Inc.**

Statement of Net Worth

SAMPLE Inc. Assets		ME, Inc. Assets	
Current Assets		**Current Assets**	
Cash & Savings	$2,000	Cash & Savings	$_____
Reserves (GICs, CTBs, CSBs, etc.)*	$10,000	Reserves (GICs, CTBs, CSBs, etc.)*	$_____
Other	$0	Other	$_____
Total Current Assets	$12,000	Total Current Assets	$_____
Investment Assets		**Investment Assets**	
Stocks	$18,000	Stocks	$_____
Bonds	$5,000	Bonds	$_____
Mutual Funds	$20,000	Mutual Funds	$_____
RPP/Company Pension**	$35,000	RPP/Company Pension**	$_____
RRSPs	$7,000	RRSPs	$_____
Other	$0	Other	$_____
Total Investment Assets	$85,000	Total Investment Assets	$_____
Personal Assets		**Personal Assets**	
Principal Residence	$360,000	Principal Residence	$_____
Furnishings	$40,000	Furnishings	$_____
Vehicle	$20,000	Vehicle	$_____
Other	$0	Other	$_____
Total Long-term Assets	$420,000	Total Long-term Assets	$_____
TOTAL ASSETS	**$517,000**	**TOTAL ASSETS**	**$_____**

Statement of Net Worth

SAMPLE Inc. Liabilities		**ME, Inc.** Liabilities	
Current Liabilities		Current Liabilities	
Credit Cards	$3,000	Credit Cards	$_____
Installment Loans	$7,000	Installment Loans	$_____
Other	$0	Other	$_____
Total Current Liabilities	$10,000	Total Current Liabilities	$_____
Long-term Liabilities		Long-term Liabilities	
Principal Residence	$280,000	Principal Residence	$_____
Vehicle	$7,000	Vehicle	$_____
Other	$0	Other	$_____
Total Long-term Liabilities	$287,000	Total Long-term Liabilities	$_____
TOTAL LIABILITIES	$297,000	TOTAL LIABILITIES	$_____
Assets – Liabilities $517,000 – $297,000		Assets – Liabilities $_____ – $_____	
NET WORTH	$220,000	NET WORTH	$_____

*   Abbreviations: GICs – Guaranteed Investment Certificates; CTB – Canadian Treasury Bills; CSBs – Canada Savings Bond

** RPP – Registered Pension Plan. Obtain your current accumulated retirement account balance or accrued annual pension amounts (estimate from your employer).

Three Crucial Signs to Measure Your Financial Wellness

1. **Statement of Net Worth** – The reservoir of money for SAMPLE Inc. includes cash and investment assets, the dollar value of property, furnishings, and vehicles. These assets are measured against the liabilities, which include credit card debt, installment loans, vehicle loans, and mortgages. The difference between the assets and liabilities is SAMPLE Inc's. personal net worth of $220,000.

Total Assets less Total Liabilities = Net Worth	
SAMPLE Inc. $517,000 − $297,000 = $220,000	**ME, Inc.** _____ − _____ = _____

2. **Current Ratio** – This ratio is calculated by dividing the current liabilities into the current assets, which in this example equals 1.2. And ideal current ratio is 1.5 to 2 or higher. Obviously, if the ratio is below one there would be a high probability of credit card or loan defaults.

SAMPLE Inc. Current Ratio = $\dfrac{\text{Current Assets} \quad \$12,000}{\text{Current Liabilities} \quad \$10,000} = 1.2$

ME, Inc. Current Ratio = $\dfrac{\text{Current Assets} \quad \$\_\_\_\_\_}{\text{Current Liabilities} \quad \$\_\_\_\_\_} = \_\_\_\_\_$

3. **Debt to Equity Ratio** – This ratio is calculated by dividing the net worth into total liabilities, which in this example equals 1.35.

SAMPLE Inc. Debt to Equity Ratio = $\dfrac{\text{Total Liabilities} \quad \$297,000}{\text{Net Worth} \quad \$220,000} = 1.35$

ME, Inc. Debt to Equity Ratio = $\dfrac{\text{Total Liabilities} \quad \$\_\_\_\_\_}{\text{Net Worth} \quad \$\_\_\_\_\_} = \_\_\_\_\_$

Note: A ratio > than 1 means assets are financed mainly with debt; A ratio < than 1 means equity provides a majority of the financing.

If the ratio is high (financed more with debt) than you face a riskier position especially if interest rates are on the rise.

Statement of Net Monthly Cash Flow

Your income is the lifeblood of your financial system and is referred to as your cash flow. Money is like a liquid that flows in as income and out as expenditures. Your money flow may be positive (more comes in than goes out) or for many people it may be negative (more goes out then comes in). The overall direction of your flow is called net cash flow. There is an unlimited source of good household cash flow calculators on the Internet that would enable you to draw up a rudimentary budget for **ME, Inc.** that will help you determine:

- Where your money comes from
- Where your money goes
- Whether you have a positive or negative cash flow

Personal Budget
ME, Inc.

Description	Monthly	
	SAMPLE INC.	ME, Inc.
INCOME		
Employment Income – Paycheque #1	$5,100	
Spouse/Partner (If applicable) – Paycheque #2	$0	
Investment Income	$0	
TOTAL INCOME	$5,100	
EXPENSES		
Savings/RRSPs/TFSAs	$500	
Mortgage/Rent	$1,450	
Home Taxes	$300	
Vehicles	$600	
Insurance – Vehicle	$160	
Insurance – Home	$50	
Insurance – Term	$100	
Credit Card Debt	$75	
Installment Loans	$125	
Utilities – Energy/Water/Electric	$150	
Telephone/Cell Phones/Wireless	$80	
Cable/Internet Service	$60	
Food – Groceries	$300	
Food – Eating Out	$160	
Entertainment	$120	
Transportation – Fuel & Maintenance	$300	
Other	$0	
TOTAL EXPENSES	$4,530	
NET INCOME	$570	

Section 2 Financial Wellness

Did You Know?

How Does My Situation Compare to "Average" Canadians?

- Canadians household debt is at extreme levels – $1.41 trillion in December 2009

- Canadians owe $1.44 of debt for every $1.00 of income (highest ratio in the top 20 developed countries) and should the economy revert again into recession many will face dire consequences

- Average debt per household is $41,740 (excluding mortgages in 2009; 2.5 x greater than in 1989).

Consider This!

- In mid-2010, about 375,000 Canadians were struggling with their current mortgage payments at a time of extremely low interest rates.
- If interest rates increase by 2%, many more Canadian families will be challenged by higher mortgage payments; many will "hit the wall" of foreclosure by their mortgagee, some will need to attempt serious debt consolidation, still others will face bankruptcy.

If you plan on being anything less than you are capable of being, you will probably be unhappy all the days of your life.
– Abraham Maslow

The secret of your success is making your vocation, your vacation.
– Mark Twain

The Science of Wealth Accumulation

Creating a Financial Plan for ME, Inc.
In your role as President and chief financial officer (CFO) of **ME, Inc.** it's your job to manage your company's financial resources – to make your wealth grow over time. Financial management is the process **ME, Inc.** can use to consolidate all aspects of your financial affairs into one coordinated plan, so that every decision can be viewed in the context of specific financial and lifestyle goals. "Know thyself" is probably the most important aspect of personal financial management, particularly our attitude with respect to the psychology of money. Money and wealth management permeates every aspect of our lives.

Why do similar families end up with very different levels of wealth? The answer to this question has a lot to do with the laws of attitude, "I can versus I can't" plus skills and the willingness to set goals, objectives, and to develop an action plan. Those who plan and develop household budgets, set priorities and develop benchmarks are therefore more likely to control spending thereby achieving their goals of wealth accumulation.

The first ingredient you need for any investment program is capital, which is simply another word for savings. Generally, capital is acquired by employing a gradual accumulation program over a period of years. It can also come from an inheritance or a sudden windfall. But for most people disciplined savings through a company sponsored pension plan or through a commitment to annual RRSP contributions and/or a regular savings program usually provides the capital for investment.

Wealth is what you accumulate – not what you spend! More savings and less consumption = greater capital for investment.

Loanership
There are two major ways for individuals to invest their capital in the marketplace. One way embraces "loanership" securities, which could be defined as money you would lend to a bank or trust company in the form of a savings account, from which you expect to earn the posted savings rate on your account in return for lending your money. Similarly, as a bondholder or loaner you expect to be paid a specific amount of interest every year until the bond matures.

Loanership generally offers three advantages:

1. You know that your capital is safe – the amount you put in is what you can expect to get back.
2. Lending your money to the bank provides a reliable stream of income in the form of interest.
3. You have quick access to your cash – a characteristic called liquidity.

Ownership
The second way to invest is with "ownership" securities, which, in contrast, bring different rewards and risks. As a shareholder or owner of a company you share in the firm's success or failure as the price of its securities fluctuates with changes in the company's financial performance, industry developments, and the economy. You are also entitled to vote in the election of directors and receive any dividends declared. Another form of ownership is the purchase of real estate, such as owning your home as opposed to renting your dwelling.

When you buy stock in a company, you own part of a business whereby you share in all those things that go into a living, breathing operation: employees, unions, markets, customers, competitors, technologies, and so on. That means you get to share in the good times and the bad times. True, there is risk involved, but the rewards of equity ownership can be great.

What is Equity?
The term equity comes from the total value of a corporation beyond any debts it may owe, those debts being the ownership interest of a company held by its common and preferred shareholders. The word equity or shares is synonymous with the common and preferred stocks held by these shareholders. You will note that we often refer to common and preferred shares as equity or stocks.

Case Profile: Mohamed Abboud, age 37 –
Fixed Income versus Equity Returns
Mohamed joined the IT department of a large multinational technology company 10 years ago and expects to retire in 25 years at the age of 62. He is a member of his employer's pension plan and his contributions

along with the match by his company, he expects could average $400 per month throughout his 35 year working career. Dependent on how Mohamed invests his capital, his results will be very different.

Mohamed expects his total combined pension contributions will amount to $168,000. As a fixed income (loaner) receiving a rate of return of 5% his capital will grow to $456,331; as an equity (owner) earning a return of 9% his capital will grow to $1,185,539. The difference of $729,208 is the potential additional reward that he will receive for assuming the risks of investing in equities. Mohamed believes the wisest approach to managing his pension assets is to allocate his money equally – 50% fixed income and 50% equities. This course of action could generate a 7% return or $724,624 during his working career.

The Sleep Factor

One of the most important questions every investor needs to ask is, "What is my sleep factor?" Because, if the investment you choose in the pursuit of your desired investment return, carries a level of risk that causes you to worry and thus affects your sleep, then you have to reassess whether the rate of return you desire is achievable from investments that you would be comfortable holding in your portfolio.

Consider This!

One of the best ways to go about accumulating wealth is to study how the rich became wealthy and then model or copy their success:

- They set goals and have a commitment to financial planning.
- They pay themselves first and have a cash management system.
- They live within their means and seek value for purchases.
- They are committed to the preservation of capital.
- They purchase insurance to protect their loved ones.
- They increase the return on their investments based on their risk tolerance.
- They actively plan tax avoidance and tax deferral strategies.
- They maintain an appropriate fixed income to equity ratio.
- They distribute capital among investments in each asset class.

Though no one can go back and make a brand new start, anyone can start from now and make a brand new ending.
– Carl Bard

Some people don't believe they're having a good time unless they're doing something they can't afford.
– Unknown

What is Your Risk Tolerance?

Every CFO is responsible for managing the investment risks their company could face. Similarly, as the CFO for **ME, Inc.** you need to determine what your comfort zone is with respect to risk? To find out the answer to this question, you have to get to know yourself financially. What kind of investor are you? What does your personal risk tolerance profile look like? What is your financial attitude toward savings versus investing and the risk/reward trade-off? Complete Your Risk Tolerance Profile to find out.

ME, Inc. Risk Tolerance Profile

Instructions: *Statements 1–6 should be answered on the basis of how strongly you agree or disagree with each statement, assuming you have a long-term investment timeframe.*

Questions *7–10 measure risk tolerance based on which statements you choose.*

Statement	Strongly Agree				Strongly Disagree
	A	B	C	D	E
1. I want a guarantee of income from my investments, even if I have to accept a lower yield.	☐	☐	☐	☐	☐
2. I can't afford any possible loss of capital regardless of the potential return.	☐	☐	☐	☐	☐
3. I am satisfied with my yield from TDs, GICs, CSBs, T-bills, and bonds, so I would rather not invest in the volatile stock market.	☐	☐	☐	☐	☐
4. I am concerned that my present savings level will not provide the necessary income to offset the long-term effects of inflation.	☐	☐	☐	☐	☐
5. I want a blend of safety, income, and growth right now and for my retirement years.	☐	☐	☐	☐	☐
6. My greatest concerns are inflation and taxes, therefore I am willing to invest for maximum protection from these arch enemies.	☐	☐	☐	☐	☐

Question	Risk Tolerence				
	A	B	C	D	E
7. An investment you made six months ago turned sour and currently is showing a 30% decline. How would you respond? a) Sell and cut your losses. b) Do nothing and wait for a rebound. c) Buy more and lower the average cost of your investment.	☐	☐	☐		
8. Given the following situations, which would you choose? a) $1,000 cash now. b) A 50% chance of winning $3,000. c) A 20% chance of winning $10,000. d) A 10% chance of winning $25,000.	☐	☐	☐	☐	
9. If you were faced with two potential losses, which would you choose? a) A 100% chance to lose $2,000. b) An 80% chance to lose $3,000.	☐	☐			
10. Which situation would you prefer? a) Investment in money market vehicles that prevented you from losing 40% of your capital in a market correction. b) Investment in equities that double your money.	☐	☐			

Here are the points earned by each response. Circle your responses and total your score.

	Points				
	A	B	C	D	E
Q 1	A1	B2	C3	D4	E5
Q 2	A1	B2	C3	D4	E5
Q 3	A1	B2	C3	D4	E5
Q 4	A1	B2	C3	D4	E5
Q 5	A5	B4	C3	D2	E1
Q 6	A5	B4	C3	D2	E1
Q 7	A1	B3	C5		
Q 8	A1	B3	C4	D5	
Q 9	A5	B1			
Q 10	A1	B5			

Your Total Score : _____

What kind of investment personality do you have?

10–20 points: Very Conservative (Risk-Avoider) – Level 1

If you scored 20 or under points, you are likely a very conservative investor. Safety of capital is very important to you, so risk is something you prefer to minimize or even avoid altogether. Variability in your investments is not something you enjoy, and you are prepared to accept lower returns as a trade-off for being sure your capital is guaranteed. The type of product you favour is probably savings accounts and cash equivalents such as money market funds, T-bills, CSBs, TDs, and GICs.

21–30 points: Conservative (Risk-Minimizer) – Level 2

At 21 to 30 points, you are still quite conservative. Instead of totally avoiding risk, however, you are likely comfortable with a small bit of risk, but will try to minimize its effect. You favour the same products as the very conservative personality, but would also be comfortable with bonds and debentures, preferred shares, and some high-quality blue-chip common shares for income.

31–40 points: Growth-Oriented (Risk-Blender) – Level 3

Between 31 and 40 points, you are a "risk-blender." You are less conservative than those who scored lower points, and you would like to see some growth in your portfolio. You will always have some conservative products in your portfolio. You will also want to have a good selection of common shares or mutual funds invested in stocks to achieve the desired growth in your investments. You might include a wide range of investment vehicles in your portfolio, including aggressive common stocks, foreign and global equity mutual funds, some convertible shares, warrants, and perhaps a tax-sheltered investment.

41–50 points: Speculative (Risk-Taker) – Level 4
The highest scores on this questionnaire indicate that you are not only comfortable with risk, but also welcome it when you believe it will create the conditions for achieving the growth you seek. While your portfolio will have some cash and blue-chip stocks in it, you may lean toward more speculative common shares, options, futures, precious metals, certain higher-risk real estate investments, and special situations.

Risk Tolerance Profile Analysis
Your investment decisions are personal and will reflect your goals, needs, attitudes, and philosophy.

Three factors will impact the amount of money you accumulate for retirement:

1. How much money you save.
2. How long your money is invested.
3. The rate of return you earn on your investments.

Investment Planning Timeframes
The shorter the timeframe for an investment, the greater the need to be ultra conservative choosing reserve instruments that are liquid and that can be converted to cash in one year or less, e.g., Canadian Treasury Bills (T-bills), Canada Savings Bonds (CSBs), term deposits, money market funds, etc.

Conversely an individual who is a member of a company-sponsored pension plan with a lengthy career until retirement would want to assume greater growth prospects by embracing a mix of bonds and perhaps an even greater emphasis on equities dependent on the individual's comfort zone with respect to risk.

When You Plan For	Select Investment
1 Year	Cash Reserves
2 Years	Fixed Income (short term)
3 – 5 Years	Balanced or Diversified
6 – 10 Years	Equities
A Lifetime	Knowledge

Did You Know?

Entrepreneurs are risk takers, willing to roll the dice with their money or reputation on the line in support of an idea or enterprise. They willingly assume responsibility for the success or failure of a venture and are answerable for all its facets.

— Victor Kiam

Consider This!

Three Steps to Consider Before You Invest

1. The first and most important step is to identify your goals: how much you'll need and when you'll need it.
2. The second step is to understand your comfort zone or tolerance for risk.
3. The third step is to be clear about your investment timeframe.

Risk comes from not knowing what you're doing.
— Warren Buffett

You can measure opportunity with the same yardstick that measures the risk involved. They go together.
— Earl Nightingale

Instead, to be financially free, we need to learn how to make mistakes and manage risk.
— Robert Kiyosaki

Asset Allocation Strategies

One of the most important considerations in managing your finances is asset allocation – how to allocate your assets. There are four things that you can do with your money and investments: buy assets, sell assets, change title to assets, or do nothing.

Without a financial plan you cannot make effective saving, investment, or asset allocation decisions. Just as a chief financial officer invests in new buildings and equipment for a business, an investor constructs an investment portfolio. Your mission as the CFO of **ME, Inc.** is to design a portfolio mix tailored to fit your risk tolerance and timeframe. And the eventual success of your portfolio depends on your asset mix and its tax implications.

What is Asset Allocation?
Asset allocation is a process of distributing investment capital to various asset classes to meet the investor's changing needs for income, liquidity, and growth.

The three major asset classes are:

- **Reserves –** These may include savings accounts, treasury bills, short-term deposits, and other liquid investments that can easily be converted to cash
- **Fixed Income –** This may include GICs, bonds and debentures, mortgages, strip coupons, and other fixed income vehicles
- **Equities –** These may include preferred shares, common shares, equity mutual funds, and exchange traded funds.

Other asset classes include materials (base metals); commodities such as food, water, and energy; precious metals such as gold, silver, and platinum; and real estate.

What Every Investor Needs to Know
The two most important things every investor needs to know:

- the investment risk profile
- the investment timeframe

As an investor, your mission is to design an investment portfolio mix tailored to fit your comfort zone for risk and your investment timeframe. The asset allocation you choose for your portfolio evolves from your three major investment objectives of liquidity, income, and growth. And the three major asset classes of reserves, fixed income, and equities meet these investment objectives very well. Each asset class accommodates particular investments suitable for the purpose of measuring risk versus reward, and return on investments. Each of the investment selections produces a range of risks and rewards, generally, the greater the risk, the greater the reward.

Major Objective	Asset Class	Investment	Major Risk	Major Reward
Liquidity	Reserves	T-bills	Long-term Inflation	Liquidity
Income	Fixed Income	Bonds	Mid-term Volatility Long-term Inflation	Fixed Maturity Value
Growth	Equities	Stocks	Short-term Volatility	Protect Purchasing Power /Inflation Hedge

Remember, the eventual success of your portfolio depends on your asset mix and the varying taxes you'll owe for interest income, dividends, and capital gains.

Just as a chief financial officer invests in new buildings and equipment for a business, an investor constructs an investment portfolio. Your mission as the CFO for **ME, Inc.** is to design a portfolio mix tailored to fit your risk tolerance and timeframe.

What have the historical average annual returns been for the three major asset classes?

Asset Class		Percentage Returns as at 6/30/2010			
		3 Yr	10 Yr	20 Yr	60½ Yr
Reserves	T-bills (Cash)	1.6%	2.8%	4.4%	5.8%
Fixed Income	5-year GICs	2.6%	3.2%	5.0%	7.0%
	Bonds	7.4%	7.8%	10.2%	7.5%
Equity	S&P/TSX Composite Total Return Index	-3.9%	3.3%	8.4%	10.1%
	S&P 500 Total Return Index CDN $	-9.8%	-4.8%	7.2%	10.8%
	World Markets ex US TRI CDN $	-12.2%	-2.3%	4.2%	10.7%
Inflation (Consumer Price Index)		1.3%	2.0%	2.0%	3.8%

Source: Andex Associates Inc., a Morningstar Company

Investors will note that over the long term, equities have outperformed bonds by 3% to 4% annually, whereas during the short term, bonds have provided greater returns. Much of this return was created by capital gains from bonds as interest rates plummeted from their double-digit peak levels in the early 1980s to the lowest levels reached in the late 2000s during the Great Recession. You might also note how the Canadian stock market has outperformed the US and World market Indices significantly during the last 10 years.

Did You Know?

The three most important ingredients to success are:

1. Time
2. Consistency
3. Patience

The individual investor should act consistently as an investor and not as a speculator. This means that he should be able to justify every purchase he makes and each price he pays by impersonal, objective reasoning, that satisfies him that he is getting more than his money's worth for his purchase.

– Benjamin Graham

The safest long-term investment for the preservation of purchasing power has clearly been a diversified portfolio of equities.

– Jeremy Siegel,
  Finance Professor Wharton School of
  the University of Pennsylvania

Employer Pension Plans 101

Are you one of the fortunate Canadian employees who enjoy the benefits of a company-sponsored pension or savings arrangement? If so, you are absolutely blessed because only about one third of private and public sector employees have a registered pension plan (RPP) and perhaps up to another third share in some other type of savings arrangement.

What type of pension plan do you have?

Let's begin by taking a look at the major types of employer-sponsored plans: defined benefit (DB), defined contribution (DC), group RRSP, deferred profit sharing plan, and supplemental employee retirement plan.

Defined Benefit (DB) – Traditionally, DB plans have been the most common type of pension plan arrangement for employees and they provide the following features:

- a clearly defined benefit
- retirement income based on a formula that includes your earnings history and length of service
- a secure predictable income stream
- professional management

Other features can include early/postponed retirement benefits, indexing, survivor benefits before and after retirement, and forms of pension (more on these later).

Perhaps the greatest benefit of a DB plan is that the benefit is predictable. Employees have the peace of mind in knowing that their individual pension income will be based on a formula. All of the investment decisions are made by professionals and in the event of a pension shortfall the employer carries the risk.

Defined Contribution (DC) – This is a pension savings plan also known as money purchase.

Major features include:

- typically both the employer and employee contribute a defined percentage of salary
- usually the employee must decide how to invest the money in the plan although some sponsors offer a single balanced plan that is professionally managed and therefore does not require the employee to be an armchair financial quarterback
- the lump sum accumulated at retirement will depend on how long the money was invested and the rate of return earned within the plan
- at retirement, monies can be transferred out of the plan to purchase an annuity (fixed income) or a life income fund (LIF)
- the lifetime annuity income will depend on contributions, earnings history, and interest rates at the time of purchase

During the last two decades most employers have opted to sponsor DC plans or Group RRSPs in the process of transferring more of the responsibility to the employees and less on the employer.

Group RRSP – This is simply a collection of individual RRSPs where the employer arranges for employees to make contributions through regular payroll deductions on a pretax basis. Some of the major benefits include flexibility (easy way to save), least costly with low management fees, easy to administer, and least regulated.

More Plan Features
Survivor benefits – If you have a spouse when you retire, the DB or DC pension must be paid as a joint and survivor pension unless you and your spouse waive this right. This enables your surviving spouse to receive a lifetime pension after your death that will be at least 60% of the monthly pension that was paid to you.

Optional forms of survivorship are:

- joint and survivor pension of 66-2/3%, 75%, 80%, or 100%
- can only be elected by married members and cannot be changed once the pension commences
- provides lifetime pension for the spouse based on the percentage elected

- surviving spouse continues to receive the pension if he or she later becomes the spouse of another person
- survivorship is not transferable and is only payable to the spouse named at commencement of the pension

Guaranteed life annuity – This life annuity is paid for the lifetime of a person or for a certain period, whichever is longer but in any event for a minimum such as 5, 10, or 15 years. This option can be elected by single or married members (spouse must sign a waiver form). Upon retirement, the guarantee period commences and cannot ever be changed, however the guarantee is transferable.

Deferred Profit Sharing Plan (DPSP) – This plan is an employer-sponsored plan registered with the Canada Revenue Agency that enables the employer to share the profits made from the business with all employees or a designated group of employees.

Contributions can only be made by the employer and are not taxable to the employee until withdrawn. Savings can be taken out in a lump sum or installments for up to 10 years. Lump sum payments can be transferred tax-free to a RPP, RRSP, or RRIF.

Supplemental Employee Retirement Plan (SERP) – These plans are provided by many plan sponsors as part of their total rewards package to assist individuals in the higher income brackets that are not able to make the full 18% contribution to their retirement funds due to limits in the Income Tax Act. SERPs can be unfunded (base promise), funded, or secured with a letter of credit, investment trust, or insurance vehicles.

How much is your employer pension plan worth?

Assume a plan member has a fixed pension income of $2,500 per month ($30,000 per year). How much money would need to be invested and at what rate of return to deliver $30,000 of income per year assuming the retiree lived for three to four decades in retirement? As can be seen from the chart below the amount of capital required is dependent on the rates of return that are earned. For example, if you assumed that you could consistently earn an average return of 6% on your capital than the capital required to produce a $30,000 income stream is $500,000.

Rate of Return		Capital Requirement		Retirement Income
4%	X	$750,000	=	$30,000
5%	X	$600,000	=	$30,000
6%	X	$500,000	=	$30,000
7%	X	$428,571	=	$30,000
8%	X	$375,000	=	$30,000

Of course the design of a fixed income annuity pension is based on a payback of principal and interest for the duration of one's retirement. Imagine an employee who retires at age 60 and lives for 34 years in retirement. This person would receive $30,000 times 34 years = $1,020,000. Annuity payments are calculated based on average life expectancies (mortality tables). It's a game of numbers – those who live a long time end up being subsidized by those who live a shorter lifespan.

Employees who work for an employer who sponsors a pension or savings arrangement are fortunate indeed when they reach the doorstep of retirement.

Benefits of Belonging to an Employer-sponsored Plan

There are many benefits for employees who have the privilege of belonging to an employer's pension plan. First and foremost it provides a disciplined forced savings plan for one's retirement. In fact, research conducted by Transamerica Center for Retirement Studies found that the availability of a plan is highly correlated to proactive savings behaviours that go beyond simply providing a vehicle to save. Their research showed:

- Employees who are offered a plan start saving at an earlier age than those without a plan, giving them more years to contribute and the potential to grow greater assets.
- 77% of employees offered access to an employer plan take advantage, while just 57% of those not offered a plan save outside of work.
- 61% of employees in company-sponsored plans are more likely to have a retirement savings strategy compared with just 40% of those without an employer-funded plan.

- 78% of workers with access to a workplace plan feel that they understand asset allocation principles, compared with 53% of those who don't have a plan.

In general employees who belong to company-sponsored plans exhibit more proactive retirement savings behaviours, demonstrate higher levels of knowledge about retirement investing, and are more confident in their ability to retire comfortably.

Management Expense Ratio (MER)

The second major benefit of an employer-sponsored plan is the cost savings in the management expenses because of the economies of scale that can be offered in a plan covering hundreds, perhaps thousands of plan members. Many employer plans have extremely low MERs in the range of 0.35% to 0.65% whereas mutual funds in the retail market have averaged: equity funds of 2.50% and bond funds of 1.70% over the last two decades.

Case Profile: David Irving, age 30 Invests in Mutual Funds (retail) and Charles Kerr, age 29 Invests in his Employer's Pension Plan (institutional).

David Irving and Charles Kerr have known each other since grade school. David runs a very successful flower shop business and his friend Charles is a banker.

Assume David makes $500 per month RRSP contributions in mutual funds for 30 years—equities 50% and bonds 50% — that deliver a combined gross return of 8.50% less MERs of 2.10% for a net return of 6.40% or $563,512.

Assume Charles also invests $500 per month into his employer-sponsored plan and also achieves a gross return of 8.50% less MERs of 0.50% for a net return of 8.00% or $755,616.

As can be seen in this example, fees will have a huge impact on the total assets accumulated for these two investors. Because Charles is privileged to have the opportunity to invest in his employer-sponsored pension plan, which charges fees 1.60% less than David's RRSP over the 30-year period, he will be able to accumulate an additional $192,104 more than his friend David prior to his retirement.

Section 2 Financial Wellness

Reality Check on Fees

Have you ever considered how great the erosion is on your investment returns due to the impact of management expense ratios (MERs)?

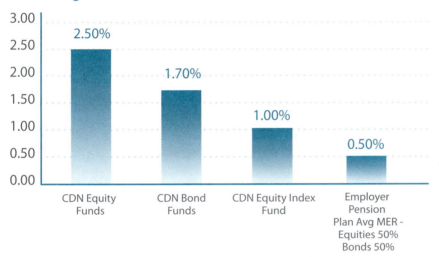

So how would the expenses in this chart affect the long-term accumulated results for an investor?

$500 Per Month Invested for 30 Years with an assumed annual equity market return of 10% and bond market return of 7% less MERs, compounded monthly.

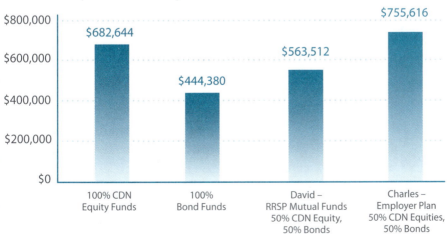

Did You Know?

Five Key Retirement Risks

There are five key retirement risks we will explore in depth in later lessons but to give you a heads up now they are:

Longevity – As life expectancy increases, you have a one in four chance of being alive at age 94.

Health – Tremendous technological advances enable us to live longer but the bigger question that will need to be answered is, "what is your quality of life?"

Financial – You may need to embrace the ownership of equities for growth in the early years of your retirement to protect your purchasing power for a retirement that could last longer than your working career.

Inflation – How will you protect your purchasing power that erodes over time?

Cash flow – Studies have shown that 4% is a sustainable long-term withdrawal rate and you may need to be ultra conservative in your early retirement years so as not to deplete your pension assets.

We'll have a lot more to say about the major retirement risks later.

Consider This!

We often ask the question in the Institute's seminars to employees approaching retirement within a few years, "What is the largest asset you own?" Most participants respond, "My house." The reality is that employees with 25-, 30-years or more of plan membership often have accumulated pension assets with a greater value than their homes.

You don't get what you deserve – you get what you plan for!
– Unknown

What is Your Wealth Accumulation Philosophy?

The thesis of **ME, Inc.** is to think about your personal finances as though they comprise a business. The objective is to get you to apply the same discipline and focus as you would if you were running a company – because you are: **ME, Inc.** Be mindful that a CFO who lacks focus or the skills or the discipline to get on with his or her job will not likely succeed. Neither will the head of **ME, Inc.**

Take a look at these trigger words in the illustration below to see how they might help you in your quest for financial peace of mind – key words like *choices* – personal choices that you make in every aspect of your life; and the struggle to find a *balance* in the process. When it comes to investing the operative word is *courage* which is required to invest with *discipline* and *focus*. What is your *attitude* with respect to the stock market? Do you have the *knowledge* and the *skills* to create a plan of *action* to meet your goals? And what is your belief system and *philosophy* about money, health, relationships, and your retirement?

Implement Your Own Strategy

So what would be an appropriate asset allocation strategy for you? Of course your objectives will change dependent on what stage you are at in your life cycle. Investors in the wealth accumulation phase early in their careers might be more concerned with growth while investors in the wealth distribution phase that are drawing an income from their investments might be more concerned with the short-term need for liquidity and income. And they are also mindful of the need to continue to improve their return on investment (ROI) to offset the ravages of inflation to protect their purchasing power.

> **When it comes to investing the operative word is *courage* which is required to invest with *discipline* and *focus*.**

Asset Allocation Risk Tolerance

The first step required to determine an asset allocation strategy based on risk tolerance is to complete Your Risk Tolerance Profile (earlier lesson in this section).

Once you have scored Your Risk Tolerance Profile and determined your personal risk tolerance level you can review the smorgasbord of investment options for each risk profile versus that of a typical professionally managed corporate pension plan, which allocates its assets to address the needs of all plan members at every stage of the life cycle both during the wealth accumulation and distribution years, i.e., its mandate is to meet the needs of all employees in their 20s, 30s, 40s, 50s, 60s, as well as all of its retirees.

Compare below the asset allocations of the various risk tolerance profiles versus that of a typical pension plan which invests 3% reserves, 35% fixed income, and 62% equities.

These percentages for each risk tolerance profile are not cast in stone – feel free to increase or decrease 5% to 10% within any of these categories. These asset allocation guidelines give you a range of investment alternatives of the four basic risk types outlined in Your Risk Tolerance Profile questionnaire.

Asset Allocation Comparison
Wealth Accumulation Phase – During Career

Asset Class	Typical Pension Plan	Risk-Avoider	Risk-Minimizer	Risk-Blender	Risk-Taker
Cash & Money Market	3%	0%	0%	0%	0%
Bonds	35%	70%	50%	30%	15%
Equities – Canadian	32%	15%	25%	35%	43%
Equities – U.S.	15%	7%	12%	17%	21%
Equities – International	15%	8%	13%	18%	21%

Wealth Distribution Phase – During Retirement

Asset Class	Typical Pension Plan	Risk-Avoider	Risk-Minimizer	Risk-Blender	Risk-Taker
Cash & Money Market	3%	15%	10%	5%	0%
Bonds	35%	70%	60%	45%	30%
Equities – Canadian	32%	8%	15%	25%	35%
Equities – U.S.	15%	3%	7%	12%	17%
Equities – International	15%	4%	8%	13%	18%

Our observations from the two charts above are:

- the allocations for the typical pension plan remain the same for each comparison
- during career the risk blender profile aligns most similarly with the typical pension plan
- during retirement the risk-avoider, risk-minimizer, and risk-blender profiles are all more conservative in their asset allocation strategies than the typical pension plan which is invested for a cross section of all investor profiles and for all seasons – both during the accumulation and distribution phases

Did You Know?

Most millionaires share a common trait – they're frugal! Millionaires live well below their means and make savings for investments their number one priority. Individuals, who don't follow this basic rule, rarely achieve wealth.

Tell your money where to go; instead of asking where it went.
– Unknown

The best time to plant a tree was 40 years ago.
The second best time is today.
The same advice applies to investing!
– The Financial Education Institute of Canada

SECTION 3
INVESTMENT MANAGEMENT
The Basic Essentials

The Magic of Compound Interest

Money multiplies itself through the accumulation of compound interest. Compounding measures the worth of your investment when you add the annual interest earned to the principal amount. Interest payments get bigger and bigger because the amount that the interest payments are calculated on has become larger. A quotation attributed to Baron Rothschild said, "I don't know what the Seven Wonders of the World are, but I know what the eighth is: compound interest."

A compound return on equities would include the reinvestment of dividend income and the growth of the security.

How Productive is Your Factory?
Imagine you own your own financial planning factory **ME, Inc.** It may be your sole ownership or perhaps it is a business shared between you and your spouse. There will only be two ingredients to input into your factory – money and time. Imagine your savings are the money input and the magic of compounding is the time input.

What you do with these two ingredients inside your factory; how you manage, manipulate, or massage these two inputs will determine your output; something we'll call comfortable retirement. And your comfortable retirement might begin at age 58, 62, 67, 70 or any age depending upon how well you have run your factory.

Don't forget, this applies to everyone whether you are as many as 30 years or as few as 5 years away from retirement. You are building a rest of your life plan.

Over a 35-year career, an increase of 1% in the annual rate of return on your pension will deliver a pension payout that's 20% greater at retirement.

Are you satisfied with the level of production in your financial planning factory?

Factory Production Comparisons

Timeframe	Return on $1,000 Investment (Compounded Annually)		
	Factory A 3%	Factory B 6%	Factory C 9%
1 Year	$1,030	$1,060	$1,090
Annual Return Earned	$30	$60	$90
Factory B & C divided by Factory A		2 x greater	3 x greater
Compounded Return – 30 Years	$2,427	$5,743	$13,268
Less Original Investment	$1,000	$1,000	$1,000
Net Return Earned	$1,427	$4,743	$12,268
Factory B & C divided by Factory A		3.3 x greater	9.3 x greater

Imagine three individual factories producing different rates of return at 3%, 6% and 9% on a $1000 investment compounded annually. On the surface, after one year of production, the rate of return is basically two times and three times greater in factories B and C respectively over the return in factory A.

"I don't know what the Seven Wonders of the World are, but I know what the eighth is: compound interest."

Now let's take a look at the magic of compounding after 30 years of production. Factory B producing a 6% return is 3.3 times greater; and factory C producing a 9% return is a whopping 9.3 times greater than factory A producing at a 3% level.

Case Profile: David Higgins, age 59
David has been employed for 28 years with an electronics company in the parts department where he currently earns $75,000 annually. His employer offered a company-sponsored defined benefit (DB) pension plan when he started his career but after 10 years of service the company

switched the DB plan to a defined contribution (DC) plan whereby he could contribute up to a maximum of 10% of salary with a company match on the first 4%.

David figures his income has averaged about $60,000 per year since the DC plan was established and his career pension contributions with company match has been approximately $4800 annually ($400 monthly).

With the onset of the Great Recession, David received an incredible shock when he reviewed the decline in the value of his portfolio from quarter to quarter during 2008 and 2009. He decided to ascertain what his return would have been over the history of his DC plan for the past 28 years assuming various rates of return.

Return on $400 Invested Each Month with Interest Compounded Monthly

Details	Factory A 5%	Factory B 7%	Factory C 9%
1 Year	$5,352	$5,415	$5,478
Pension Contributions	$134,400	$134,400	$134,400
28 Years	$295,003	$420,723	$612,772

At June 30, 2008, David's DC plan was valued at $605,434 so he was pleased to see that his allocation of 40% fixed income/60% equities over the years had been providing close to a 9% return. However, between June and December 2008 the S&P/TSX index declined from 14,292 to 8,058, a loss of 43.6% and his portfolio had declined from $605,434 to $458,919 – a net decline of $146,515 or a loss of 24.2%.

This was a significant decline that occurred within a very short timeframe. Had this happened earlier in David's career it would have been easier to absorb because he would have had lots of time to recover, however, he had hoped to retire within the next two years. Now he is uncertain what he will do and when he will retire – much will depend on the duration of the bear market. In the interim David is preparing himself to accept a slightly lower standard of living and/or possibly considering part-time work in retirement.

Power of Compounding Monthly, $5 per day at 7% Growth Per Year Until Age 65

The following chart illustrates the value of compounding $5 per day for 10, 20, 30, and 40 years until age 65. Share the magic of compounding with your adult children, nieces or nephews, or any other young person you know.

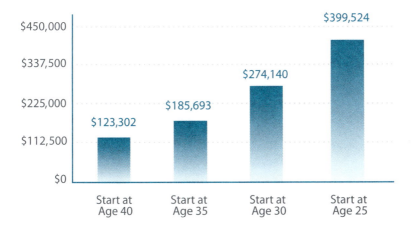

Did You Know?

Benefits You Get from Having a Planned Program of Savings:

- Financial independence in retirement
- Contingency fund for emergencies/problems
- Source of funds to capitalize on opportunities
- Emotional security/peace of mind
- A model of prudent financial behaviour for your children
- Opportunity to leverage your personal wealth through compounding

Remember that money is often a prolific generating nature. Money can beget money, and its offspring can beget more.
— **Benjamin Franklin**

The most powerful force in the universe is compound interest.
— **Albert Einstein**

Impact of Interest Rates on Bond Prices

When new bonds are issued they pay a fixed rate of interest called a coupon rate until the bond matures. The price at which a bond will trade depends on the quality of the issue, current interest rates, the maturity date, the number of bonds available for trading (the liquidity of the issue), and other factors.

The most important consideration when trading bonds is the outlook for interest rates. Interest rates and bond prices have an inverse relationship – when interest rates go up bond prices go down; and when interest rates go down bond prices go up. The reason for this is simple. When interest rates drop those bonds with a coupon (interest) rate higher than the rates currently available in the market become more attractive. Investors are willing to pay more to have their money earn a higher rate of interest.

For example, assume you own a $1,000 bond paying 5% interest. Now imagine interest rates go up and a new bond issue offers 6% interest. Your bond is not as attractive to an investor who can earn more interest by purchasing the new bond. Therefore, in order for your bond to be of value to a prospective purchaser it will have to trade at a discount from its current price to a point where it would yield 6% similar to the new bond. Conversely, if interest rates fall to 4%, your bond would become more valuable and trade at a premium because an investor would earn more money from your bond with a 5% coupon than the newly issued bond with a 4% coupon.

Interest rates and bond prices have an inverse relationship– when interest rates go up bond prices go down; and when interest rates go down bond prices go up.

The market prices of long duration bonds fluctuate more than shorter bonds due to interest rate risk. Therefore, the longer the bond maturity the greater the risk and the potential impact on bond prices. Of course, if you plan to hold the bond to maturity for the steady income that it provides, then the change in price would not matter to you.

Bond Prices and Interest Rates

Did You Know?

Long-term bonds typically offer higher rates of return than short-term bonds. Why? Because the longer the term, the greater the risk and the bond purchaser wants to be compensated for the time risk.

Consider This

The 7% Solution

What do the financially independent top 7% of the population do that the other 93% don't do?

- They pay themselves first by saving 10% or more of their gross income.
- They set clearly defined goals and create an action plan.
- They acquire financial knowledge and expertise.
- They invest for the long term with stable, low risk, blue chip stocks with a history of dividend payments.
- They use other people's money to help grow their wealth. Homes are acquired with borrowed money (mortgages) and investments can also be financed by investing. However, they make sure they understand the risks/rewards involved.

Money must be managed — you are the steward of every dollar that comes your way.

– The Financial Education Institute of Canada

Risk versus Chance

The real wealth long-term performance record of common shares far outstrips savings accounts, bonds, and other fixed-income assets. Since 1950, Canadian stocks have outperformed fixed-income bonds by 3% to 4% (depending on one's tax bracket) after adjusting for taxes and inflation.

Do not permit the superior performance of equities to camouflage the inherent risks within the market, nor should you confuse risk with chance. Risk can be measured and calculated, chance cannot. Successful investment planning involves taking some measured degree of risk. In general, as you increase your degree of risk you increase your potential reward. What are some of these risks?

Interest rate risk is the relationship of market price to interest rate and is always the inverse for fixed-income investments – when interest rates fall, bond prices go up; and when interest rates rise, bond prices decline.

Interest rates ↓ Bond prices ↑
Interest rates ↑ Bond prices ↓

For equity investments, rising rates usually mean inflation is also on the rise. In the initial stages of an expanding economy, the price of stocks may also rise with the general boom. If however, the rise in interest rates is very high or prolonged, companies suffer because borrowing becomes more expensive, sales slowdown, and profits decline as the economy, over time, falls into recession. The sale of shares in anticipation of a weaker economy is the primary cause of falling stock prices.

Market risk is the uncertainty in the future price of stocks that arises from a change in investor attitudes toward the markets. This change in investor psychology may cause a market to decline regardless of any fundamental changes affecting the companies being traded on the market. Rumours of war, international tensions, a change in government, concerns over fiscal and/or monetary policy, and many other events can influence investors to sell en masse. Ownership securities are always subject to market risk.

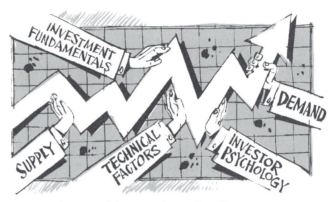
Investor psychology – negative or positive will impact both the bond and stock markets

Political risk involves changes in tariff and subsidy policies, tax increases, government instability, interest-rate policies, quantitative easing (unlimited printing of new currency), nationalization of industries and changes in the taxation of dividends and capital gains and can affect investment values.

Financial or business risk occurs when there is some doubt about whether you will be able to collect future returns and therefore an investment may decline in value. These doubts are driven by things such as poor management, unfavorable economic conditions, increased competition or outdated technology, to mention a few.

Liquidity risk is the danger that you will not be able to sell your investment without significant delays or costly penalties. Commercial real estate would be an example of the type of investment that lacks liquidity.

Volatility risk pertains to investments (stocks in particular) that do not grow in a smooth upward fashion; rather they behave in an erratic manner featuring peaks and valleys.

Inflation risk is also known as purchasing power risk and is perhaps the greatest risk of all as it erodes the value of your investments or a stream of income on an ongoing basis. There are only two ways to offset the ravages of inflation – equities and real estate – therefore all sound financial plans should include one or both of these ownership investments.

Purchasing Power

In 20 years the **PURCHASING POWER** of a dollar would decline to just **$0.44**

Inflation has averaged 3.8% per year since 1950.

Risk can be measured and calculated, chance cannot. Successful investment planning involves taking some measured degree of risk.

Degrees of Risk

There is no such thing as a riskless investment. There are only degrees and types of risk. Fixed-income investments such as treasury bills, GICs, and bonds are subject to purchasing power risk as well as interest rate risk, both of which can be greater than the market risk involved in a well-balanced portfolio or a professionally managed equity fund.

Your degrees of risk can vary greatly. Many people think that by saving in a bank or trust company, by purchasing term deposits, GICs, or fixed-income vehicles they are completely safe. In reality, you are actually going broke safely by losing ground to inflation and taxes. For example, if you were earning 5% on a bond and your marginal tax rate was 40% you would have a net return of (5%-2%) = 3%. If inflation was at its historic long-term average of 3.8% you would be losing 0.8% on your capital or purchasing power!

While there is no risk to your original capital in this example, you have no real gains; you have merely lost purchasing power. No gains, no headway! Contrast that example to a 10 year record on an equity mutual fund. There are many professionally managed mutual funds that would have produced high single-digit to low double-digit returns over the long term.

Did You Know?

Creative risk taking is essential to any goal where the stakes are high. Thoughtless risks are destructive, of course, but perhaps even more wasteful is thoughtless caution, which promotes inaction and promotes failure to seize opportunity.

There is no security on this earth. Only opportunity!
– Douglas MacArthur

Don't be afraid to go out on a limb. That's where the fruit is.
– H. Jackson Browne

The only person who never makes mistakes is the person who never does anything.
– Dennis Waitley

It wasn't raining when Noah built the ark.
– Warren Buffett

Put the Power of Dividends to Work for You

Savvy investors know that taking a long-term approach to building their investment assets over many years will eventually work in their favor. They do not allow themselves to succumb to fear and panic selling when the mood of the market turns negative. And these investors know that in a declining market, stocks that pay dividends have a distinct advantage over those that don't, because they pay quarterly cash distributions and inevitably avoid the worst blows of a bear market.

There is nothing mysterious about the stock market's ability to grow over time. Good solid companies that have the ability to increase their sales and revenues, most often experience positive growth in earnings, which can be reinvested in new growth opportunities and/or paid out to shareholders with dividends. These companies are rarely glamorous or exotic – usually they are large blue-chip stocks often referred to as "widows and orphans" in mature industries such as banks and utilities.

> **Sophisticated investors intuitively know that the road to positive returns is through ownership of a diversified portfolio of equities that has the potential to deliver capital appreciation from the growth of earnings, and through a sustainable long-term growth in dividend income.**

Virtually every long-term study of total returns indicates that dividends account for approximately two thirds of gains. A recent study of the benchmark S&P 500 index over a 50-year period compared simple stock price appreciation with gains made by reinvesting any dividends paid. The results were astounding: the S&P 500 capital appreciation was 381%; its dividends reinvested gains were 905% which supports the fact that dividends accounted for 70% of the overall return.

Historical Dividend Yields
Historically, when dividend yields were below 3% they were considered bearish; and when yields were above 5% they were bullish. Sometimes, when yields are extremely low, companies use their cash to buy back shares in order to reduce their capitalization thereby creating fewer shares outstanding and therefore greater earnings and potentially

larger dividend payouts for the remaining shareholders. When yields are extremely low the buyback of shares often represents the best use of a corporation's excess capital. One of the best entry points to invest is after the market has suffered a severe setback causing the price earnings ratios to decline and the dividend yields to increase substantially. Whenever dividend yields rise above 5% and assuming the earnings are quite stable, history has proven this is a good time to invest.

Dividend Yields

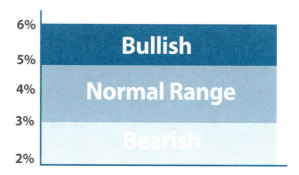

Case Profile: Cynthia Chin and Monica Chang
Let's take a look at how two long-term investors fared using different strategies to invest $10,000 capital beginning in January 1999.

Cynthia Chin fancied herself as an ultra conservative investor who had a very low risk tolerance. Cynthia opted to invest $10,000 in a 5-year Guaranteed Investment Certificate (GIC) yielding 5% in January 1999. In 2004, when the GIC came due, Cynthia reinvested her $10,000 capital into a new 5-year GIC yielding 3.5%; and when it came due in 2009 she reinvested $10,000 once again into a new five-year GIC yielding 2.6%. As you can see the interest rates had been declining during this time.

Cynthia Chin – $10,000 5-Year GIC

Purchase 5-Year GIC	Amount of Investment	Yield
January 1999	$10,000	5.00%
January 2004	$10,000	3.50%
January 2009	$10,000	2.60%
January 2014	$10,000	?%

Monica Chang became somewhat of a student of the market through self-study and by taking a basic financial planning course as one of her electives while at university. Monica's comfort zone enabled her to take a risk-blended approach with respect to her investments. She was well aware that dividend-yielding stocks could provide the ultimate inflation hedge and they were the investment of choice for some of the world's greatest investors of all time (John Templeton, Walter Schloss, and Warren Buffet). Monica decided to invest in Royal Bank stock and her initial $10,000 purchase enabled her to acquire 522 shares at a price of $19.14. The dividend on Royal Bank was $.46 per share in January 1999, and yielded 2.4% (dividend divided by market price equals yield).

Monica Chang $10,000 Royal Bank – 522 shares at $19.14 / share

Description	January 1999	January 2009	% Change
Price	$19.14	$36.10	89%
Dividend	$0.46	$2.00	335%
Yield	2.4%	5.5%	129%
January 2009 yield based on 1999 cost price			10.4%
Dividend returns 25% greater than interest after-tax			1.25
Comparative Interest Equivalent Yield			13.0%

At the time of purchase in January 1999, the yield on the 5-year GIC was 5% versus the yield on Royal Bank shares of 2.4%, therefore on a yield basis the GIC was more than twice that of the Royal Bank shares. However during the 10-year period ending January 2009, Royal Bank increased its dividend from $0.46 to $2.00 dollars per share with one or more dividend increases most years. By January 2009, Royal Bank was trading at $36.10 with a dividend of $2.00 per share and a yield of 5.5%. However, what would the yield be on the original purchase that Monica made in January 1999 at $19.14 based on the January 2009 dividend of $2.00 ($2.00 divided by $19.14 equals 10.4%). And since Canadian dividends are taxed more favorably than interest income; dividends generate higher after-tax returns than interest earned on GICs and other fixed-income investments. The interest equivalent yield that Cynthia's GIC would need to earn to be comparable with the Royal Bank shares is 13%.

Investor Summary January 2009	Cynthia GICs	Monica Royal Bank
Price	$100	$36.10
Yield	2.60%	5.5%
Yield on 1999 Price	2.60%	10.4%
Capital Value	$10,000	$18,844
Current Market	GICs	Royal Bank
Current Price	$100	
Capital Value	$10,000	

And finally let's take a look at what happened to each investor's capital. Cynthia's $10,000 GIC still has a current value of $10,000 however the purchasing power of her capital would be substantially less today due to inflation. Monica's $10,000 investment in Royal Bank grew from $19.14 in January 1999 to $36.10 in January 2009 therefore her 522 shares increased in value to $18,844. As we go to print in the fourth quarter of 2010, Royal Bank is trading in excess of $55 per share or valued at more than $28,700 – not bad when you consider the market has suffered through two severe bear markets in both the early and late 2000s.

Dividend Factoids

- Corporations that pay dividends usually indicate a quality company.
- Dividends tend to increase rather than decrease over time; and dividend increases are a sign of confidence in the company's future.
- The Board of Directors has a strong aversion to increasing a dividend if there is even a minimal chance of having to decrease it at a later date.
- When dividends are increased investors obtain an insider view of management's thinking.
- Generally predictable – the last thing a company with a historically stable dividend will do is cut its dividend because it would change the shareholder base and the company would risk losing some of its conservative value investors.
- During market declines, dividend-paying stocks decline less, and perform better than non-payers.
- Canadian dividends are more favorably taxed.
- Increasing dividend payments over time provides the ultimate hedge against inflation.

Consider This!

Dividends Matter

Virtually every long-term study of total investment returns indicates that dividends account for almost two thirds of gains.

– *Investors Chronicle*

I only ask one thing of my money. Work hard like I do. That is why 97% of positions I own pay me a dividend or have yield.

– *Kevin O'Leary, Chairman, Gencap Funds LP*

Do you know the only thing that gives me pleasure? It's to see my dividends coming in.

– *John D. Rockefeller, (1839–1937)*

The risk of being out of stocks, in the long run, is greater than the risk of owning them.

– *David Dreman, Contrarian Investment Strategies: The Next Generation*

How to Harness Inflation

Since 1950, Canada has experienced inflation in 57 out of 60 years. Since 1955, Canada has had inflation every year until the Great Recession began in 2008. In early 2010, inflation was benign and the greater fear of deflation is uppermost in the minds of many politicians throughout the world. Many countries are using every stimulus tool at their disposal to avoid a deflationary economy by lowering interest rates and applying quantitative easing by keeping their printing presses running 24/7/365.

History has shown that in most cases you have to "own instead of loan" in order to accumulate wealth and retire with financial security. Why? Because the economies of the world are more likely to experience growth and inflationary conditions over the long term in the future just as they have in the past. Therefore, the question each investor needs to ask is, "Am I prepared to beat inflation?"

Are you prepared to beat inflation?

Ask yourself:

- How are my savings and investments distributed today?
- Am I a saver (loaner), an investor (owner), or both?
- Are my Canada Savings Bonds, term deposits, guaranteed investment certificates, and other money market instruments protecting me from inflation?
- How much time am I prepared to spend on learning more about investments through e-learning, reading financial publications, newsletters, attending seminars, and taking investment courses?
- And finally, how much capital am I prepared to invest at regular intervals to grow my wealth accumulation plan?

The effect of income taxes on wealth accumulation is well known. But, when coupled with the ravages of inflation, many investors are left with little or no return. During the decades of the 1970s and 1980s most people lost 2% to 3% of their real purchasing power each year. But there were measures they could have taken to stay ahead of inflation.

Put Inflation to Work for You

Inflation redistributes wealth. It hurts the elderly and those on fixed income, but it can help those who have financial resources and choose to harness its energy. In an inflationary environment such as the period of the early 1980s, you could have accumulated a lot of money if you had sufficient capital.

You can be either a victim of inflation or its beneficiary. If you learn to substitute the word dilution every time you see the word inflation, you will come to have a better understanding of inflation.

If you are a saver placing your savings in a "guaranteed" position, you are a gambler, and if the past is any indication of the future, you are guaranteed to lose.

Think in terms of a total portfolio positioned efficiently at the proper time to beat inflation. Your portfolio must maximize your after-tax return, balanced against a level of risk that provides you with peace of mind.

Inflation – Victim or Beneficiary?

Let's look at inflation two ways – you can be either a victim or a beneficiary of inflation.

The following chart depicts the scenario. The centre line of the chart shows inflation at 4% because of the fact that over the last 60 years inflation has averaged, about 4%.

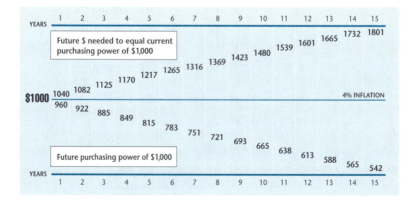

The Victims
Of all pensioners, aged 65 or older, 35% have less than $20,000 income to report. Picture a retired person on a fixed income of $1,000 per month. Assume a 4% inflation rate. Now look down the road 10 years when, due to inflation the purchasing power of the $1,000 buys only $665 worth of goods.

Many people don't know where they stand with regard to their future pensions, let alone how to plan. They move through their working years; age 60 to 65 arrives and they find themselves, quite suddenly, on the "victim" side of the inflation scenario.

> **Inflation redistributes wealth. It hurts the elderly and those on fixed income, but it can help those who have financial resources and choose to harness its energy.**

The Beneficiaries
On the other side of the coin are inflation's beneficiaries. They may be people like you who are gainfully employed. You have income, you're able to save 5%, 7%, 10% of your salary, and you really are starting to work hard to put money aside, especially during the last 7 to 10 years of your career.

Picture yourself with the same $1,000, and put it to work in the various asset classes. Imagine you purchase some fixed-income bonds yielding 5% and some equities returning 9%. With the Canadian dividend tax credit and special treatment for capital gains, the return could be in the high single digits, perhaps 7% or 8%. Those who can harness inflation and put it to work through wise investments are inflation's beneficiaries.

Did You Know?

Real return bonds are bonds that pay a rate of return that is adjusted for inflation. This feature assures the investor that purchasing power will be maintained regardless of the future rate of inflation.

Real return bonds pay interest semi-annually based on inflation-adjusted principal, and at maturity they repay the principal in inflation-adjusted dollars.

Consider This!

Income Lifestyle Requirement with Inflation at 4%

If you earned $30,000 a year in 2000, by 2010 your annual salary would have to be $44,407 just to maintain the same purchasing power you had in 2000. By 2020, that $30,000 salary will have to jump to $65,734; and by the year 2030, $97,302.

Inflation is like sin; every government denounces it and every government practices it.
– Fredrick Leith-Ross

Law of inflation: whatever goes up will go up some more.

How to Diversify Your Portfolio

Diversification is a strategy that enables an investor to reduce risk by dividing capital between asset categories and within asset categories. The first step an investor needs to consider is which asset categories to choose.

Asset Categories

Asset class – The most common asset classes that investors choose to diversify their portfolios are: reserves (cash), fixed income (bonds), and equities. Historically, equities have been the best performing asset class most years. However, some years bonds are best and occasionally cash and cash equivalents are best. The theory of holding multiple asset classes is that when one class is doing poorly, another class is doing well, and therefore diversification reduces the overall risk for the investor. Some investors also include real estate, commodities, and precious metals asset classes in their portfolios.

Geographic region/country – Diversifying a portfolio by acquiring securities from around the world can minimize the effect of a negative development that is contained in one region/country.

Currency – Owning a basket of currencies is a prudent way for investors to offset the potential erosion in the buying power of the Canadian dollar.

Management style – The three most common styles for equity investing are value, growth, and sector rotation. By combining these styles in their portfolio investors insulate themselves from the worst effects of economic conditions that don't favor one particular style.

Diversification Within Asset Categories

After a portfolio has been diversified among asset categories the next step is to diversify within each category. For example, one of the asset categories investors could choose is asset class and one of the subsets of asset class is equities. The next question investors would need to answer is how to diversify their portfolio with equities. For instance, should they own individual stocks, stock mutual funds, or exchange-traded funds?

Asset Categories	Asset Allocation	Investment Strategies
Asset Class	Reserves	Cash, Savings, CSBs, Treasury Bills, Term Deposits, Money Market
	Fixed Income	GICs, Mortgages, Bonds – Government, (Federal, Provincial, Municipal) Corporate, and Term (short, medium, long)
	Equities	Stocks, Mutual Funds, Exchange-Traded Funds
	Real Estate	Income Property, REITs
	Commodities	Food, Energy, Water, Materials
	Precious Metals	Gold, Silver, Platinum
Geographic Region /Country	Region – Asia, Europe, Latin America, Emerging Markets	Countries – China, Japan, Australia, US, UK, Brazil, India, Russia etc.
Currency	Region (Euro)	Countries – Japan (yen), China (renminbi), Swiss (franc), Brazil (real), etc.
Management Style	Value, Growth, Sector Rotation	Large, mid, or small capitalization, top down versus bottom up

Many investors choose equity mutual funds to provide a measure of safety by dividing their money into a wide cross-section of securities. This would be impossible to do on their own unless they had hundreds of thousands of dollars to invest. Instead of putting all of their eggs in a few baskets they are able to enjoy the benefits of many baskets. Depending on their size equity mutual funds generally hold anywhere from 30 to 300 different stocks in many industries.

Case Profile: Alex Chin and Gregory Chang
Safety by Diversification – 20-Year Results

Alex Chin: Guaranteed Investment Certificate	
$50,000 @ 5%, 5-Year GIC	$132,500
Gregory Chang: 5 Equity Mutual Funds	
$10,000 @ 0%	$10,000
$10,000 @ 2%	$14,900
$10,000 @ 8%	$46,600
$10,000 @ 10%	$67,300
$10,000 @ 12%	$96,500
Total	$235,300

Section 3 Investment Management – The Basic Essentials

It may seem hard to understand that a properly diversified portfolio having some investments invested in asset classes that are losing money today is an essential element of prudent investment management.

Let's take a look at the results that two different investors achieved over a period of 20 years. Alex Chin chose to invest $50,000 in GICs and averaged a 5% return over 20 years and grew his portfolio to $132,500. During the same time frame Gregory Chang divided his capital into five equal parts and purchased 5 equity mutual funds featuring different management styles and geographic regions. His returns varied between 0% and 12% over 20 years and eventually grew to $235,300 or $103,300 greater return then Alex. Note that even though two of Gregory's mutual funds under-performed substantially, generating returns of 0% and 2% respectively, the other three funds returning 8%, 10%, and 12% performed very well enabling his diversified portfolio to substantially outperform Alex.

Investment Portfolio Flow Chart

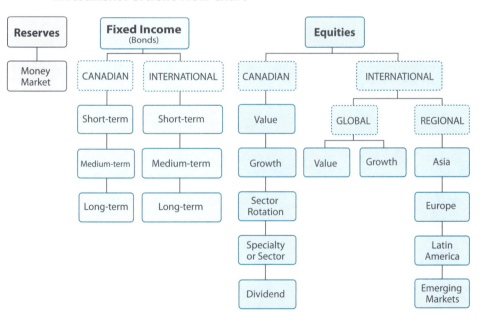

Diversification 101
A properly diversified portfolio blends asset categories into various asset classes and investment strategies that have low co-variances, which means while some decline in value others will tend to advance. Putting all of your eggs in lots of different baskets isn't enough; an investor should also select baskets that do not move in tandem.

It may seem hard to understand that a properly diversified portfolio having some investments invested in asset classes that are losing money today is an essential element of prudent investment management. Many investors have difficulty coming to terms with this discouraging truth because they are predisposed to feel losses much more painful than gains. Worse still, many investors react emotionally to any negative performance and impatiently sell losers to chase winners in their portfolio, often at the most inopportune time. They forget that the essence of sound Diversification 101 demands a continual exposure to the losing asset classes of the day. Why? Because today's losers will become tomorrow's heroes.

Consider This!

Many investors understand the need to diversify, however they do so in a haphazard way. The key to diversifying successfully is to structure your holdings to suit your investment goals and objectives, being mindful of your comfort zone with respect to risk.

It is not enough to invest in many securities, it is necessary to avoid investing in securities with high co-variances among themselves.

– Harry Markowitz

If you're in your 20s, hooray if you're already thinking about retirement. Your diversification can tilt a little more toward aggressive investments. However, if you're a Baby Boomer you have to be more conscious of volatility because you have a shorter time period.

– Claire Saunders

Mutual funds have historically offered safety and diversification. And they spare you the responsibility of picking individual stocks.

– Ron Chernow, Author

Dollar Cost Averaging

Dollar cost averaging is the greatest tool at an investor's disposal for a long-term investment program. The concept of dollar cost averaging suggests that the best way to invest is by a systematic program of equal amounts over a reasonable period of time.

This tool can also be used for packaged investments such as professionally managed mutual funds or exchange-traded funds. Most packaged products provide an automatic dividend reinvestment plan (DRIP) feature at regular intervals to enable maximum compound growth of the investment.

Imagine that you are investing $100 a month in a specific mutual fund if the price per unit of the fund is $10, that month's investment will buy you 10 units.

Dollar-Cost Averaging

Term	Investment	Price Per Unit	Units Bought
Month 1	$100.00	$10.00	10.000
Month 2	$100.00	$6.00	16.666
Month 3	$100.00	$9.00	11.111

Suppose that when your next month's installment is due, the units dropped to $6 each; that month you by 16.6 units. If the fund value increases to $9 dollars per unit in the third month, your $100 buys 11.1 units.

Therefore, during the three-month period you have bought a total of 37.78 units for a cost of $300. At a current value of $9 dollars, your units are worth almost $340, or over 13% more than you invested.

Three-Month DCA Summary

Total Cost	$300.00
Units Purchased	37.778
Current Price	$9.00
Current Value of Investment	$340.00
Capital Gain (Loss) 13.3%	$40.00
Increase (Decrease) in unit value .... (10.0%)	($1.00)

Section 3 Investment Management – The Basic Essentials

Even though the units have dropped to $9 dollars from $10, you are ahead in your accumulation program, because you actually bought more units at a lower price than at the higher price. If you had purchased all of the units at the $10 price, your capital would actually have decreased by 10%.

Dollar cost averaging is the greatest tool at an investor's disposal for a long-term investment program.

Dollar cost averaging takes the worry out of knowing when to invest by encouraging a steady pace over the long run. With dollar cost averaging you gradually acquire a larger and larger block of units, assuring that the most units are bought when prices are lowest, because your money goes farther, and the least number of units are bought when prices are highest. It is even possible to buy fractional units so that you buy only what you can afford when you can afford it. That means smart conservation of financial energy. And when you dollar cost average over the long term, your portfolio will probably do better than relying on a buy recommendation at a specific point in time.

Dollar Cost Averaging Examples Under Different Market Scenarios
$100 per Month Plan for 10 Years

Down and Up Market

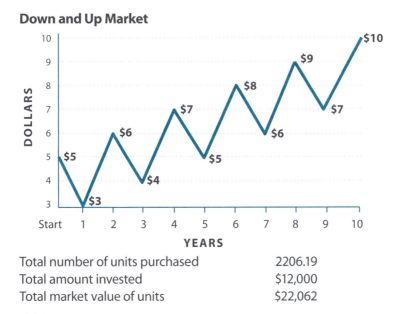

Total number of units purchased	2206.19
Total amount invested	$12,000
Total market value of units	$22,062

This investor bought units between $3 and $10 over 10 years and during down markets accumulated more units, which resulted in a lower average cost per unit.

Up Market

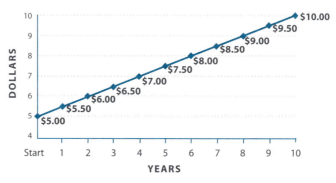

Total number of units purchased	1725.05
Total amount invested	$12,000
Total market value of units	$17,250

This investor bought units over 10 years at steadily increasing prices between $5 and $10 and thus participated in a long-term advancing market cycle instead of sitting on the sidelines hoping for a more opportune time to invest.

Down Market and Return to Original Value

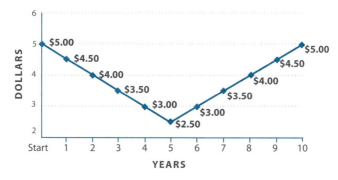

Total number of units purchased	3339.06
Total amount invested	$12,000
Total market value of units	$16,695

This investor bought units at $5 down to $2.50 and back to $5 over 10 years and was able to benefit from dollar cost averaging by increasing the market value of the units by $4,695 in spite of the fact that the units never traded above the original market price.

Case Profile: Karen Fisher and Cheryl Gordon

Consider the example of two friends, Karen and Cheryl. Karen begins a Registered Retirement Savings Plan (RRSP) at age 30. For eight successive years she invests $300 per month ($3,600 per year). Her investment grows at the rate of 8% per year. After the eighth year, Karen leaves work to become a homemaker and no further investments are made.

Cheryl does not begin her retirement savings contributions until she is 38 (the age at which Karen stopped her contributions). Cheryl invests $300 per month ($3,600 per year) until age 65 at the same 8% growth each year.

You can see the incredible result in the table below. Karen, who contributed earlier with only eight years of contributions, ends up with more money than Cheryl, who made 27 years of contributions.

This is the power of compounding over time. The difference in the two investors' results is that Karen's compounding had an eight-year head start. Those early years were worth more than the entire 27 years of later contributions made by Cheryl and provided her with more financial peace of mind when she reached retirement. You might show this one to your kids!

Year-End Value

Age	Karen Fisher		Cheryl Gordon	
	Annual Investment	With Compound Interest	Annual Investment	Year-End Value
30	$3,600	$3,760	$0	$0
31	$3,600	$7,832	$0	$0
32	$3,600	$12,242	$0	$0
33	$3,600	$17,018	$0	$0
34	$3,600	$22,190	$0	$0
35	$3,600	$27,792	$0	$0
36	$3,600	$33,858	$0	$0
37	$3,600	$40,428	$0	$0
38	$0	$43,784	$3,600	$3,760
39	$0	$47,418	$3,600	$7,832

	Karen Fisher		Cheryl Gordon	
Age	Annual Investment	With Compound Interest	Annual Investment	Year-End Value
40	$0	$51,353	$3,600	$12,242
41	$0	$55,615	$3,600	$17,018
42	$0	$60,231	$3,600	$22,190
43	$0	$65,231	$3,600	$27,792
44	$0	$70,645	$3,600	$33,858
45	$0	$76,508	$3,600	$40,428
46	$0	$82,858	$3,600	$47,544
47	$0	$89,736	$3,600	$55,250
48	$0	$97,184	$3,600	$63,595
49	$0	$105,250	$3,600	$72,634
50	$0	$113,986	$3,600	$82,422
51	$0	$123,446	$3,600	$93,023
52	$0	$133,692	$3,600	$104,504
53	$0	$144,789	$3,600	$116,937
54	$0	$156,806	$3,600	$130,403
55	$0	$169,821	$3,600	$144,986
56	$0	$183,916	$3,600	$160,780
57	$0	$199,181	$3,600	$177,884
58	$0	$215,713	$3,600	$196,408
59	$0	$233,617	$3,600	$216,470
60	$0	$253,007	$3,600	$238,197
61	$0	$274,006	$3,600	$261,727
62	$0	$296,749	$3,600	$287,210
63	$0	$321,379	$3,600	$314,808
64	$0	**$348,053**	$3,600	**$344,697**
	Less Contributions Invested	$28,800	*Less* Contributions Invested	$97,200
	Total Capital Growth	**$319,253**	**Total Capital Growth**	**$247,497**

Benefits of a Monthly Plan

- Establish an annual contribution amount
- Budget for minimum monthly contributions
- Average cost of units purchased
    - low prices = more units
    - high prices = fewer units

The value of dollar cost averaging removes the decision-making "guesswork" from when to buy units thus permitting volatility to work in your favour.

Did You Know?

Why Use Dollar Cost Averaging?

The basic motivation for using dollar cost averaging is to develop a mechanical strategy that does not require investor decision-making. It is mostly a psychological technique for overcoming fear and greed.

Consider This!

Closest Thing to a Foolproof Investment Formula

Dollar cost averaging is the closest thing to a foolproof investment formula if three essential ingredients are present:

1. You must have the financial ability to continue your program when the market declines. Welcome each inevitable decline as a fortunate opportunity to buy more shares at lower prices, which reduces your average cost.
2. Assuming that the future will be no better than the past, (just not worse), then every period of temporarily declining prices will eventually be followed by a period of rising prices and this is all you need to assure a profitable long-term venture.
3. Patience, patience, patience – is all you need provided your investment contributions are directed to packaged investments – only a widely diversified, carefully selected and professionally managed portfolio is reasonably assured to participate in a general market rise.

Wealth creation is a process, not an event!
– The Financial Education Institute of Canada

The Two Market Forces You Need to Follow

Much has been written about economic cycles and market psychology. Many theories have been developed by investors who call themselves "fundamentalists" and "technicians." Don't believe that any one discipline or theory presents the full picture. Consider all the data available and choose the one or a combination that works best for you.

In the first place, the price of anything can go up or down in response to one or more of three elements only:

- Demand for the product or service
- Supply of the product or service
- Value of the dollar

The first rule for investment success is based on the economic law of supply and demand:

- When demand increases, supply decreases and markets move up.
- When demand decreases, supply increases and markets move down.

There are two market forces that every investor needs to consider prior to making a decision to buy or sell any investment such as stocks, bonds, or real estate.

1. The economic law of supply and demand for a business enterprise – simply means that whenever there is more supply than demand for a company's products or services, prices will usually be affected negatively because of the lack of sales and excess inventory buildup. Conversely, when there is more demand for a product or service, this will lead to increasing sales and often an improvement in earnings and potential price appreciation in the company's stock.

In a severe recession businesses suffer from the lack of demand and depending on the severity of the cycle the following chain of events can occur: typically prices will decline to lower levels, then inventories are sold off at fire sale prices; and if the conditions worsen employees are laid off and at the extreme the business may have to close one of its divisions or worse still, file for bankruptcy.

2. What level are interest rates in the economy and which direction are they likely to head next? Typically, lower interest rates provide a stimulus for growth in the economy whereas higher rates tend to slow things down. In the face of global recession most governments attempt to re-inflate their economies by adopting low interest rate policies. Low interest rates are generally considered positive or bullish for the stock market, while higher interest rates are negative or bearish.

There are two market forces that every investor needs to consider prior to making a decision to buy or sell any investment such as stocks, bonds, or real estate:

1. **The economic law of supply and demand**
2. **What level are interest rates in the economy.**

Consider This!

No one really knows for sure what direction the economic environment and the markets will embark upon.

If your major concern is an inflationary economy you will want to own hard assets such as natural resources, real estate, and/or stocks.

If however, your major concern is a deflationary economy then reserves, cash, and short-term money market instruments and/or short-term bonds will be your best bets.

Therefore the best hedge for either of these possibilities might be an investment selection that includes equal allocations to both equities and bonds – a 50/50 mix.

Only buy something that you'd be perfectly happy to hold if the market shut down for 10 years.

– Warren Buffett

Money is good for nothing unless you know the value of it by experience.

– P.T. Barnum

Section 3 Investment Management – The Basic Essentials

What is the "Best" Investment?

It seems everyone you talk to knows the best investment, but no one agrees on the same answer. Is a size 9 shoe a "good" shoe? Only if it fits your foot. Is 7% a "good" return on investment? Only if it fits your objectives.

Suppose you need a 7% percent return on investment to get everything you want and the government issues Canada Savings Bonds paying 3% interest guaranteed for 8 years. Is this a good investment? Perhaps, but not for you. You cannot achieve your objective of a 7% growth rate – guaranteed!

On the other hand, if you know you need a 7% return, you care little which investment you have your money in as long as it earns 7% or more.

By now you have probably realized there is no set method or formula to accomplish your investment strategies. However a model called the Rate of Growth of Investable Capital (ROGI) does a good job of addressing the savings and investing process.

First let's look at all the ways you can increase your wealth – all two ways!

- Increase your savings
- Increase your return on investment

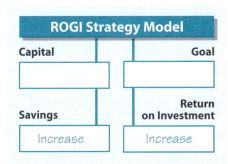

There are only three ways to increase savings; and three ways to increase your return on investments. You can increase your savings

93

by: earning more, spending less, and paying less income tax. You can increase your return on investment by: taking more risk, educating yourself to make better investment decisions, and hiring professional management.

However, you should be aware that taking more risk and/or hiring professional management does not come with an ironclad guarantee. Sometimes taking greater risks or choosing the wrong advisor could also lead to a decrease in your return on investment.

The core message that you the President of **ME, Inc.** can take away from this exercise is:

1. You should have a plan.
2. Stay disciplined and stick to the plan.
3. Try to avoid the worst errors.

The ROGI Strategy Model is operated by plugging in three values so that you can determine the fourth.

Suppose you have $10,000 today and in one year's time you need to have $12,000. To reach that figure, your investable capital must be increased by $2,000 or 20%. Here is how the ROGI Strategy Model helps to make strategy design easy.

Suppose you could save $2,000 over the next 12 months. What do your investments have to earn? The following diagram shows that the return on your investment can be 0% and you still achieve your objective of $12,000 in one year's time. You can put your $10,000 under the mattress.

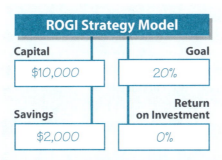

What if you invest your $10,000 at 20% for the next year? What will your savings have to be? Answer: $0. The $10,000 you invest at 20% grows to $12,000. You meet your objectives without a penny saved.

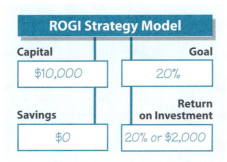

The above extremes illustrate how the model works. More typical is a situation where you save $1,000 and invest your capital at 7%. The diagram below shows that you would be $300 short of your target at the end of the first year.

What is the solution?

Imagine that you have hired a professional money manager. You want your manager to help you earn a minimum of 10% on your investment. If the money manager can do this, your savings of $1,000 together with the return on your capital will be enough to reach your target. What if you don't want to change your investments? Can you reduce your expenses by $300? If you can, that strategy will also reach your objectives. Is one solution better than the other? No, they both get the job done.

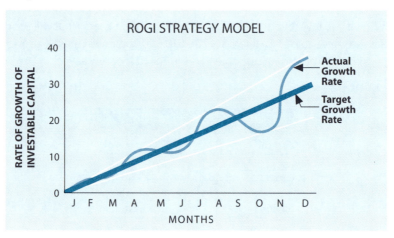

Can you think of other ideas that will get the job done? You probably can, depending upon how creative you are.

The important thing is that no matter which strategy you select for yourself, you can determine whether your goal will be achieved in one year's time by looking at the total value of your investment.

There is no "best" investment. One person's idea of a good investment may be another's idea of a gambling weekend in Las Vegas. What is more important is to identify the investment return you need in order to have everything you want, when you want it. That done, any investment that can give you at least that return is satisfactory – as long as it also allows you to sleep at night!

> **There is no best investment – as long as it also allows you to sleep at night.**

Consider This!

It has been my experience that competency in mathematics, both in numerical manipulations and in understanding its conceptual foundations, enhances a person's ability to handle the more ambiguous and qualitative relationships that dominate our day-to-day financial decision-making.

– Alan Greenspan

It only takes two things to invest successfully – having a sound plan and sticking to it. Of the two, it's the "sticking to it" part that investors struggle with the most.

– Warren Buffett

My best investment is my imagination, because it has never failed to bring me my greatest returns.

– Randy Castillo

The party line is that stocks historically have outperformed all other investment plans.

– Jim Cramer

Only Two Ways to Increase Your Real Wealth

Investing at the best of times is a challenge for most investors. And even more disconcerting is the fact that only two asset classes have the potential to increase your real wealth – ownership of equities or real estate.

Perhaps we should start by explaining the definition of real wealth, which could be defined as an investment's net return after accounting for an individual's marginal tax bracket and inflation in the economy. Neither equities nor real estate is a perfect investment all of the time. In fact, during the Great Recession as of the second quarter of 2009, these two asset classes had declined by $50 trillion on world markets from the peak in 2007. However, over the long run of many decades, equities and real estate have often been able to provide investors and homeowners with mid to upper single-digit net returns after taxes and inflation.

Two Ways to Increase Your Real Wealth

Ownership of Equities or Mutual Funds

Real Estate

Let's compare the long-term returns for the major asset classes of reserves, fixed income, and equities over the past 50 years for an investor in the upper-middle tax bracket with a marginal tax rate of 40%. We'll use Canadian investment selections including treasury bills, long-term bonds, stocks, and Toronto real estate to represent the various asset classes as shown in the following table.

Asset Class Comparisons After-taxes and Inflation

Asset Class	Reserves	Fixed Income	Equities	Real Estate
Investment Selection	90-Day CTB's	Long-term Bonds	S&P / TSX TRI	Toronto – Single Family Home
Approximate Returns Past 50 Yrs	5.5%	7.0%	10.0%	6.1%
Marginal Tax Rate – assume 40%	2.2%	2.8%	*2.0%	**
After-tax Return	3.3%	4.2%	8.0%	6.1%
Average Inflation Rate Past 50 Yrs	4.0%	4.0%	4.0%	4.0%
After-tax and Inflation Return	- 0.7%	0.2%	4.0%	2.1%

* Canada eligible dividends receive preferential tax benefits and capital gains are taxed on 50% of the gain only.

** No tax on principal residence.

As stated at the outset there are only two asset classes that have delivered real wealth net returns over the long term – equities and real estate – and they both have the potential to provide an inflation hedge to protect the purchasing power of your capital.

As you can see from the table, an investment in a reserve type instrument such as 90 day Canadian treasury bills will actually generate a negative return after tax and inflation is taken into consideration; and long-term bonds do not fare much better, barely breaking even.

Equities

Equities, on the other hand, produce a real wealth net return of 4% after-taxes and inflation. You may note that investors in lower tax brackets would earn slightly higher returns – an additional 0.25% to 0.75%.

Often times, after experiencing severe losses, some investors make irrational decisions regarding the investment mix within their pension plan or investment portfolios, by giving up and selling the equities that created the losses in their accounts, and sitting in cash or purchasing additional reserve instruments. History has shown that over the long term this would not be an appropriate strategy. In fact, it is when the stock market looks least attractive and the mood of investors is extremely pessimistic that the market is often about to turn direction and begin a positive move forward.

There are only two asset classes that have delivered real wealth net returns over the long term – equities and real estate.

Real Estate

For many Canadians the largest investment they own is their primary residence and this asset class can reduce the overall risk level of an investor's portfolio by providing a sound long-term diversification strategy. More importantly, capital gains on a primary residence are not taxed in Canada, thus enabling this asset class to deliver positive net returns to one's real wealth.

According to a report from RE/MAX, Canada, the average price of a home appreciated 264% during a 25-year period from $76,021 in 1981 to $277,000 in 2006, which works out to an annualized return of 5.31%. Another study from the Toronto Real Estate Board shows returns averaging 6.1% for single-family dwellings over the past 50 years. Real estate has delivered sound historical performance in demonstrating that it can provide a marvelous hedge against inflation thus protecting one's real wealth.

The major difference between these two asset classes is the duration of their market cycles. Stock market cycles often occur four to five years apart whereas real estate cycles are generally much longer. For example, the Toronto real estate market peaked in 1989 and then it took seven years to reach its trough in 1996 when a new market cycle began that didn't peak until 2010 (a 20-year cycle from peak to trough to peak).

Did You Know?

The cornerstone to a good long-term financial plan is diversification. The people on the Forbes annual list of the top 400 wealthiest in the world all made their money in one of two ways:

1. Ownership of companies
2. Ownership of real estate.

Your key formula is to model their success.

The best investment is land because they ain't making any more of it.

– Will Rogers

If you do not coax one dollar to work hard for you, you won't know how to make money out of $100,000.

– E. S. Kinnear

Real estate is at the core of almost every business, and it's certainly at the core of most people's wealth. In order to improve your wealth and improve your business smarts you need to know about real estate.

– Donald Trump

SECTION 4

INVESTMENT MANAGEMENT

Intermediate Tools & Techniques

Influences on Investment Returns

Asset allocation can be responsible for up to 90% of the variation in investment results according to the book *Determinants of Portfolio Performance* by Brinson, Singer, and Beebower. They discovered that asset allocation was more important than investment selection. How an investor distributes money between the three basic asset classes of reserves (cash), fixed income (bonds), and equities is more important than security selection or market timing. Unfortunately, the vast majority of investors concentrate all of their efforts on security selection and market timing which together account for less than 10% of the variation in investment return.

Influences on Investment Returns

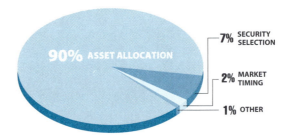

It is apparent to our facilitators when delivering the Institute's workshops that many of the participants focus on which stocks, which bonds, or which mutual funds to buy or sell, rather than concentrating on what percentage allocation they should be applying to the core asset classes, which would be based on their tolerance for risk and investment planning timeframe.

What are some of the variables you should consider in determining an appropriate asset allocation?

- Your age, stage in life, and number of dependents
- Your lifestyle dreams, goals, and values
- Your job and work income security
- Your investment objectives timeframe and marginal tax rate
- Your risk tolerance profile and the current marketplace trends (interest rates, inflation, economic conditions)
- Your investment knowledge and past experience

Now ask yourself, does your asset allocation match these guidelines based on your present stage in the life cycle?

How an investor distributes money between the three basic asset classes of reserves, fixed income, and equities is more important than security selection or market timing.

Reserves/Fixed Income to Equities Ratio

The reality of the stock and bond markets is that we don't know in which direction they will go at any point in time; no one has a crystal ball! Let's take a look at how an investor might rebalance his or her portfolio during various market cycles.

Let's further assume that an investor's risk profile suggests an ideal targeted asset mix of 50% reserves/fixed income and 50% equities.

After a strong rising equity market the portfolio mix changes to 30% reserves/fixed income and 70% equities. The equity ratio is too high for the individual's risk comfort so therefore to rebalance back to a 50% reserves/fixed income and 50% equities mix the following strategies could be utilized:

- Sell equities into strength and use the proceeds to buy reserves/fixed income
- Add new investment money to reserves/fixed income vehicles if in the accumulation phase of your life plan
- Sell equities if in the distribution phase of your life plan

Asset Mix in the Portfolio at Various Cycles

Target	Reserves/Fixed Income	Equities	Rebalance Strategy
Neutral Market	50%	50%	
Strong Equity Market	30%	70%	Sell equity into strength and increase reserves/fixed income
Weak Equity Market	70%	30%	Buy equities into weakness and decrease reserves/fixed income

The allocation most prudent investors are working with is the mid 40% range of the portfolio between the 30% to 70% or 70% to 30% range. They do not invest all of their money at the extremes such as 0% bonds and 100% equities or vice versa; that would not be conservative.

	Description	Reserves/Fixed Income	Equities
Theory:	Stock Market ↑	0%	100%
	Stock Market ↓	100%	0%
Reality:	Stock Market ↑	30%	70%
	Stock Market ↓	70%	30%

We'll discuss rebalancing strategies in a little more depth in the next section.

Asset Allocation 101

Cash (reserves) occupies a very small percentage allocation in most investors' portfolios, typically 0% to 5%. The theory behind asset allocation 101 is that investors should hold all three major asset classes at all times. Although cash usually plays a smaller role in an investor's overall asset allocation there are times when it should play a much larger role because of its near zero correlation with stocks and bonds. For example, in a market where the stock market declines by 40% what would the result be for an investor who had allocated 50% cash and 50% equities? Answer: a loss of 20%. That's why it is prudent to hold larger allocations in cash reserves under certain market conditions.

Did You Know?

Most Important Parameter

The single most important determinant of your success will be asset allocation – how your assets are distributed to the various classes of investments.

Over the longer term your returns will depend much more on what proportion of your portfolio is in equities than on what equities you have in your portfolio.

Consider This!

Crystal Ball

In theory, if you have a crystal ball and you know the stock market is going up, you would want to take advantage of this opportunity and invest 100% in equities.

Similarly, if your crystal ball indicated the market was going to go down you would want to invest in reserves and fixed income investment vehicles.

The harsh reality is that due to the lack of not having a crystal ball, prudent investors allocate money to each of the asset classes at all times to conservatively hedge their market opportunities.

A turn in the road is not the end of the road unless you fail to make the turn.
– Unknown

Ideas are a dime a dozen but the person who puts them into practice is priceless. Always remember – what you don't know will hurt you.
– Unknown

The Rule of 72

The rule of 72 is a handy tool you can use to measure the growth of your investments. Simply divide the number 72 by the annual rate of return, and the resulting figure will always equal the number of years it takes for money to double. From the chart below you can see that if you were earning a 6% rate of return on an investment, and you divide that rate into 72, your money would double in 12 years (72 ÷ 6=12); likewise a return of 9% will double your money in 8 years (72 ÷ 9 = 8).

Your money will double at an exact point by dividing 72 by the % of growth.

Rate of Return	Formula	Number of Years to Double
1%	72 ÷ 1	72
3%	72 ÷ 3	24
6%	72 ÷ 6	12
9%	72 ÷ 9	8
12%	72 ÷ 12	6

Planning for Retirement

When planning for retirement you can use the rule of 72 in reverse for example, suppose you plan to work for 12 more years before retiring and you hope to double your money by then. You can use the rule of 72 to find the rate of return you will need, to achieve this goal. Simply divide 12 into 72 to find that you will need an annual rate of return of 6% to double your money in 12 years.

Years Until Retirement	Formula	Rate of Return Required
24	72 ÷ 24	3%
18	72 ÷ 18	4%
12	72 ÷ 12	6%
8	72 ÷ 8	9%
6	72 ÷ 6	12%

Case Profile: Dominic Kovac – Rule of 72, After-tax

The rule of 72 can be used to compare tax-deferred and taxable investments. Dominic has a tax deferred Group RRSP with his employer and a taxable investment account that he manages with the help of an advisor at a local investment firm. Dominic has been earning a 9% annualized return on the Group RRSP and a lower 7% return on his taxable investment account mainly due to higher fees and management expenses.

Furthermore, Dominic's investment account is taxed at 40% and therefore his rate of return drops to 4.2% (7% X 40% = 2.8%) (7% – 2.8% = 4.2%). When you divide 72 by his rate of return on both accounts you will see that it will take Dominic 8 years to double his money in the group RRSP; and 17.1 years to double his money in his investment account.

Rate of Return	Formula	Number of Years to Double
9%	72 ÷ 9	8
4.2%	72 ÷ 4.2	17.1

As you can see from this exercise Dominic's investments are growing more than twice as fast in the Group RRSP then in his taxable investment account. When you invest in an employer-sponsored plan, you not only receive the tax-deferred benefits, but generally the management costs are much lower because of the economies of scale created by a much larger group of purchasers (wholesale) versus operating on your own as a single purchaser (retail) where fees, commissions, and management expenses are most often substantially higher. Domenic will eventually pay tax when he takes his money out of the RRSP, whereas taxes have already been paid on his investment account.

How Many Times Can Dominic Kovac Double His Money?

It is important for all investors to double their money as many times as possible, and to double their debts as few times as possible during their working careers. The first step is to determine how many years you will keep an investment before cashing it in; the second step is to divide that by the number of years it will take to double each time. Look at what happens to your money each time it doubles: $1 $2 $4 $8 $16 $32 $64.

As we saw above Dominic is currently earning a 9% rate of return on his group RRSP and he hopes to retire from the company in 24 years. How often will each $1,000 investment double in the next 24 years? A return of 9% will double his money in eight years (72 ÷ 9% = 8) therefore each $1,000 of his original investment will double 3 times to a total of $8,000.

Did You Know?

You can use the rule of 72 to measure expenses such as inflation or interest?

If the rate of inflation increases from 3% to 4% your money will lose half its value in 24 years, now 18 years

If you pay 12% on your credit cards and the rate is increased to 18% the amount you owe will double in 6 years, now 4 years.

Consider This!

Whose Interests Are Being Served?

Financial advisors and investment companies have your best interests at heart and want you to know the rule of 72 to utilize it to compound your financial success.

Lending institutions and credit card companies would rather you do not understand the rule of 72 and how their usuriously high interest rates can enslave you in a never ending compounding nightmare of servitude.

The Financial Education Institute of Canada believes that the basics of compounding, the rule of 72, and how money works should be taught to every high school student.

Investors should invest, long-term, in fundamentally sound companies. My greatest gains have been in the second to fifth years of owning a stock. Wise investors regard shares as part ownership in a company, not a lottery ticket. It takes years, not months, to produce big results.

– Peter Lynch

Inflation – The Real Story of Purchasing Power

There has been much concern about whether the Great Recession could evolve into a deflationary downward spiral. What we have witnessed from many governments globally is an initiative of decreasing interest rates and quantitative easing (the printing of massive amounts of new money) to avoid deflation at all costs. Given the choice of an inflationary versus deflationary economy the Canadian government would prefer an inflationary environment of 1% to 2% with marginal gross domestic production (GDP) in the low to mid single digits.

The last time we experienced a mild bout of deflation in Canada was the early 1950s and prior to that we had severe deflation that lasted four years during the 1930s depression era. The facts are that inflation has been the much bigger concern for our citizens over the years. Why? Inflation is the decreasing purchasing power of money over time, which is caused by increasing prices. Inflation can reduce a comfortable income to a subsistence income before its victims realize that they're in danger.

The danger is this: an average annual inflation rate of 4% would cut the purchasing power of one dollar in half in less than 18 years. Did you know that Canada's inflation rate has averaged 3.8% per year since 1950?

Effects of Inflation

If you learn to substitute the word dilution every time you see the word inflation you will obtain a better understanding of how inflation erodes the value of an investment or a stream of income over time. Let's take a look at the compound discount table for $1 as follows:

Compound Discount Table for $1

Year	Inflation Rate						
	1%	2%	3%	4%	5%	6%	7%
10	0.904	0.817	0.737	0.665	0.599	0.539	0.484
20	0.818	0.668	0.544	0.442	0.358	0.290	0.234
30	0.740	0.545	0.401	0.294	0.215	0.156	0.113

Assume you start your retirement and inflation is at 2%.

The first year your dollar buys a dollar worth of goods but next year your dollar only buys $0.98 worth and the next year only $0.96; the next year $0.94; the next year $0.92; and so on. So, let's imagine you aspire to an early retirement at age 60.

- You retire at age 60 and you live to age 80, which is 20 years.
- Twenty years later every $1 you started with, if inflation averages just 2%, will be worth only $0.67 – it will lose one third of its purchasing power.
- Now if inflation averages 4% for 20 years every dollar you start with will decline to $0.44 – it will lose more than half of its purchasing power.
- If inflation were to average 6% it will decline by over two thirds to $0.29 on the dollar.

Have you got a plan to maintain your purchasing power to offset this type of inflation in the economy?

If you learn to substitute the word dilution every time you see the word inflation you will obtain a better understanding of how inflation erodes the value of an investment or a stream of income over time.

Inflation Risk

Inflation erodes wealth therefore to offset the ravages of inflation all financial plans should include some ownership investments (equities) such as:

- Hard assets including precious metals, basic materials (copper, lead, zinc, etc.) and energy (oil and gas)
- Short-term bonds (government and corporate) and real return bonds that are adjusted for inflation
- Consumer staples (food and beverage)
- Real estate

Did You Know?

Inflation and Compounding – Some Interesting Facts

- The last year in which there was a decline in the cost of living was 2008; prior to that it was 1953.
- The highest annual inflation rate in Canada within the last century was 22.3% in 1917.
- If the annual inflation rate is 3%, it will take about 23 years for the purchasing power of $1 to be cut in half.

Consider This!

Back in 1981, a Canadian postage stamp cost 17 cents; by 2011 the same stamp cost 59 cents, an increase of 347% over just 30 years. Imagine what a stamp will cost in another 30 years.

Have you considered what investment formula you will have to pursue in order to maintain the purchasing power of your money, especially during your retirement?

By continuing a process of inflation, government can confiscate, secretly and unobserved, an important part of the wealth of their citizens.

– John Maynard Keynes

Inflation is taxation without legislation.

– Milton Friedman

Price Earnings Multiples

So, you think you would like to buy shares in a company. Is there some easy way for **ME, Inc**. to recognize a good stock? Is there some uncomplicated formula to compare different stocks? Let's look at one of the most important tools you can use to evaluate a company. The ratio of its current share price in comparison to its earnings per share (EPS), is referred to as a price earnings (P/E) multiple or ratio. Market value per share divided by earnings per share equals P/E ratio.

Example: XYZ Company is trading at $32.50 per share and the trailing EPS were $2.12 therefore the P/E ratio is 15.3. What this means is that if you buy this stock at a P/E ratio of 15.3 it will take 15.3 years for XYZ Company's earnings to add up to your original investment (to pay you back).

There are two components that affect this ratio: price and earnings.

Price —"P" is determined by investors' collective assessment of the economy and stock markets. When investors are optimistic about future returns for a company they are willing to pay more for each dollar of corporate profits and therefore their increased demand bids up the price and expands the multiple. Conversely, when investors are pessimistic demand decreases, which in turn leads to a decrease in price and a contraction in the multiple.

Earnings —"E" are determined by a company's ability to grow its earnings. Investors need to assess two types of earnings – reported or actual earnings based on the last four trailing quarters and estimated earnings projected to four quarters.

Generally, when a company's quarterly earnings have been increasing investors are attracted to a stock, and when earnings are declining investors are less interested. Investors need to be cautious when considering price-earnings multiples based on projected earnings. The risk is that if the projected earnings do not materialize investors could find themselves holding a company that is trading at a greatly inflated price.

The P/E multiple will increase or decrease based on any changes up or down in the "P" or "E". For example, in a bear market the "P" or price of a stock often declines rapidly, which lowers the multiple substantially. Other times the "E" or earnings fall off significantly thus increasing the multiple. However, the more likely scenario in a bear market is that both the "P" and the "E" would move downward over time and the P/E multiple would be in decline.

Of course when there is no "E," there is no P/E ratio to calculate. Successful investors know that earnings are the lifeblood of a company. To make money in the stock market you need to find companies that know how to grow their earnings.

The average P/E multiple for all stocks traded on the S&P/TSX in Canada during the past century has averaged around 15 times earnings. Collectively, when the average of all stocks in the index trades above 20 times earnings they are considered to be expensive and often foretell a market correction. For example, previous bull market peaks were reached when P/E multiples averaged 19 times in 1974, 23 times in 1987, and over 40 times at the peak of the technology bubble in 2000.

Normal Trading Range P/E Ratio

Conversely when the average of all stocks in the index trades below 10 times earnings they are considered to be inexpensive and often foresee better times ahead. When P/E multiples decline to the 6 to 8 times range it's a sure sign that the bear market is exhausted and the next major move will be a recovery into a new bull phase. Two major historic bear market lows occurred when P/E multiples averaged 5.6 times in 1932 and 6.6 times in 1982.

The average P/E multiple for all stocks traded on the S&P/TSX during the past century has averaged around 15 times earnings.

In the chart that follows, we have listed the market price, earnings per share, and the price-earnings ratio of five different companies. Generally speaking, the lower the P/E ratio of a company the greater the value. An investor that embraces a value style would most likely consider company D trading at P/E ratio of 5 times as a potential purchase based on its low value multiple. This does not mean that company E trading at a P/E ratio of 50 times is a bad investment – it could be a company that is a rising star within an industry that is currently in favour and another investor that embraces a growth style might select it for its anticipated future potential.

Price Earnings Ratios

Company	Market Price	Earnings Per Share	P.E. Ratio
A	$20	$1.00	20X
B	$20	$2.00	10X
C	$10	$1.25	8X
D	$15	$3.00	5X
E	$15	$0.30	50X

There are a number of additional factors to consider when analyzing a P/E ratio:

What is the P/E ratio for the broad market?

What is the average P/E ratio for the industry or sector that the company trades in? For example, a high-growth industry such as communications technology would trade at a significantly higher P/E multiple than a more conservative industry such as utilities.

What has been the long-term P/E ratio for the company and how does it compare with the current ratio? For example, if the P/E multiple were low compared with its long-term average, it might indicate that the stock is currently undervalued and therefore could be a timely purchase. Conversely, if the P/E ratio was higher than normal it could indicate that the company is overpriced.

Did You Know?

Earnings Yield

The earnings yield of a stock is calculated by reversing the equation that determines the price to earnings ratio (P/E). This is obtained by dividing what the company earns each year per share by its purchase price.

If a stock is purchased for $30 per share and it earns $5 per share, it would have an earnings yield of ($5 ÷ $30 = 16.7%). This means that the stock's value in relation to its purchase price went up 16.7% that year. The P/E ratio would be the inverse $30 ÷ $5 = 6 times multiple.

Now imagine your advisor tells you about a stock that is trading at a 6 times P/E ratio. If you are like most investors this wouldn't mean much. However, if the advisor recommended the same stock on the basis that it could earn in the vicinity of 17% you would be all ears and most likely want to purchase it.

Consider This!

The Rule of 18

If you add the long-term inflation rate to the Dow Jones price earnings ratio you get a number around 18. If the number is below 18, stocks will have an upward bias, if it's above 18, stocks will have a downward bias.

Valuations can appear dirt cheap. However, low estimated P/E ratios are only as accurate as next year's earnings forecast, which if they don't materialize, could leave investors owning a company trading at a greatly inflated price.

– The Financial Education Institute of Canada

How to Rebalance Your Portfolio

One component of designing a financial plan is to build an investment portfolio to help secure your future retirement. As part of this process the investor determines a **strategic asset** allocation mix of asset classes to deliver an expected rate of return. However, because market conditions change, a portfolio needs to be periodically rebalanced in order to maintain the long-term core allocations. As any CFO will tell you, managing **ME, Inc**. for financial wellness is an ongoing job. It is not a one-time decision, conditions change and portfolios need to be rebalanced.

Rebalancing is simply accomplished by reducing asset classes that have grown out of proportion and increasing asset classes that are underfunded, and thus by definition this process also abides by the principle to – sell high and buy low!

There are also times when an investor might want to use a **tactical asset allocation**, which is an active portfolio strategy to rebalance the percentage of assets within the asset classes, to create extra value by taking advantage of economic or market pricing anomalies or strong market sectors. Once the short-term and desired result of the tactical allocation has been achieved normally the investor will return to the core strategic asset allocation mix.

Sell High — Buy Low
Sell high and buy low sounds so simple, doesn't it? But for most investors it isn't. At market tops, greed takes over and investors believe that the good market conditions will last forever and therefore they are reluctant to sell and take a profit. Conversely, at market bottoms fear takes over and many investors end up selling at or near the bottom.

The proper approach in a declining (bear) market correction is to do one of two things: add more money to the asset class that has declined or rebalance the portfolio by selling an asset class that is high (strength) and buying into an asset class that is low (weakness).

Case Profile: Janice Dexter – Rebalance Asset Classes

Janice Dexter, aged 41, enrolled in her company's sponsored pension plan 12 years ago shortly after she joined the firm. At that time, still in her late 20s, she had limited investment knowledge and even after reading through the pension plan literature and sitting through an enrolment seminar provided by her company's group provider, she was still not comfortable with having to make choices among the funds offered by the employer plan.

For two years Janice chose to invest in the money market fund option, while she proceeded to read a few financial books and publications in an attempt to become a student of the market. At about the same time Janice had the opportunity to attend a full day workshop on financial and life planning, facilitated by an independent educational company, that was sponsored by her employer, which provided her with even more knowledge – enough to enable her to manage her employer pension more skillfully.

> **Rebalancing is simply accomplished by reducing asset classes that have grown out of proportion and increasing asset classes that are underfunded, and thus by definition this process also abides by the principal to sell high and buy low.**

So for several years now Janice has been comfortable with her pension plan allocated to the following mix: reserves – 10%, fixed income – 40%, and equities – 50%. Whenever the allocations have changed significantly Janice rebalances the asset classes by doing one of two things:

1. *She allocates new contributions to the asset class that is underweighted or*
2. *She sells into market strength the asset class that is highest and uses the proceeds from the sale to reinvest in the asset class that is weakest.*

Rebalance Asset Classes

Asset Class	Allocation %	Allocation $	Market Change	Year End Value $	Year End Value %	Rebalance $	Rebalance %	Revised Portfolio
Reserves	10%	$10,000	3%	$10,300	12.8%	($2,250)	10%	$8,050
Fixed Income	40%	$40,000	8%	$43,200	53.7%	($11,000)	40%	$32,200
Equities	50%	$50,000	-46%	$27,000	33.5%	$13,250	50%	$40,250
	100%	$100,000		$80,500	100%		100%	$80,500

During a recent two quarters, two of Janice's pension-plan allocations changed significantly. Her targeted allocations for fixed income (bonds) increased from 40% to 53.7%, while at the same time her equity allocation of 50% had declined to 33.5%. A smaller increase from 10% to 12.8% had also taken place in her reserves allocation. In order to rebalance to her original targeted allocation of 10% reserves, 40% fixed income, and 50% equities. Janice sold off $2,250 in reserves and $11,000 in fixed income and then reinvested those proceeds of $13,250 into equities at bargain basement prices marked down by 46% from the previous two quarters.

Rebalance Regularly

Most investors are not good market timers (able to beat the market consistently by switching securities or asset classes). Therefore the best way to protect themselves from succumbing to human nature is to establish asset mix ranges for their portfolios. For example, assume an investment reaches the upper limit of its range it would be appropriate to rebalance the portfolio by taking some profits to bring that investment back to the midpoint of its range and to reinvest the proceeds in another investment or asset class that is at the lower end of its range. For investors who are in a group retirement plan, you may want to think of the concept of "selling" and "buying" as making interfund transfers. And when adding new capital or directing new contributions to a different asset class they are often understood as "changing your mix for new contributions."

Asset Mix Guidelines

This sample investment portfolio illustrates various asset classes, benchmarks, and allowable ranges.

Asset Class	Benchmark	Allowable Range
Fixed Income (Bonds)	50%	40% to 60%
Equities	50% *(see subsets below)*	40% to 60%
Canadian Dividend	15%	10% to 20%
Canadian Growth	7.5%	5% to 10%
US Value	7.5%	5% to 10%
International	10%	5% to 15%
Emerging Markets	10%	5% to 15%

Did You Know?

An investor who maintained an asset balance or an allocation of 33.3% to each Canadian asset class (reserves, fixed income, equities) since 1950 would have enjoyed a 7.8% average annual return pre fees and management expenses.

To implement this type of strategy it would have been necessary to rebalance the portfolio at regular intervals (perhaps annually) to maintain the asset balance each time the asset classes diverged and grew apart.

Consider This!

Three Ways to Rebalance Your Portfolio

1. Sell investments in over-weighted asset classes and use the proceeds to acquire under-weighted asset classes.

2. Add new capital to purchase under-weighted asset classes.

3. Direct contributions for weekly, monthly, etc. accumulation programs to the most under-weighted asset class until your original portfolio balance is achieved.

Rebalancing your portfolio is one of the most important steps in investment management. Portfolios should be reviewed quarterly (more often when markets are extremely volatile) to be rebalanced accordingly if there has been significant gains or losses in any asset class.

– The Financial Education Institute of Canada

Why Big Losses Demolish Portfolio Returns

Consider the following lesson in volatility by measuring two mutual funds:

Year	Fund A		Fund B	
	% Return	$10,000	% Return	$10,000
1	26%	$12,600	12%	$11,200
2	17%	$14,742	8%	$12,096
3	-33%	$9,877	11%	$13,427
4	30%	$12,840	13%	$15,173
5	21%	$15,536	9%	$16,538
6	16%	$18,022	14%	$18,853
7	-27%	$13,156	10%	$20,739
8	22%	$16,050	9%	$22,606
9	18%	$18,939	12%	$25,318
10	19%	$22,537	7%	$27,090

Which fund would you rather own? Fund A returned 16% or more 8 out of 10 years while Fund B never returned over 14%. Fund A lost substantially in years 3 and 7 however each losing year was followed by 3 years of compounding in excess of 16%. It would seem that Fund A is the better fund, particularly in the short term. However, in actual fact Fund B outperformed Fund A by almost $5,000 over the 10-year period. Furthermore, had you invested in Fund A at the beginning of year 3 or 7 it would have taken you almost 3 years just to break even.

Big losses can demolish your portfolio returns mercilessly. Many investors don't understand the negative impact of losses versus their hard won gains. They wrongfully believe that a 50% loss this year can be recovered by a 50% gain next year to bring an investment back to break even status, however that is not the case as you can see in the following example:

The Actual Impact of Negative Returns

Initial Investment	$10,000
First Year Loss - 50%	- $5,000
Capital Available for Year 2	$5,000
Second Year Gain + 50%	$2,500
Capital Available for Year 3	$7,500
Net Loss After 2 Years	- $2,500

From the above example it is clear that to achieve success with your mutual funds investment you must avoid big losses. And the best way to prevent big losses is to buy funds with lower volatility. Be mindful, however, that low volatility does not necessarily guarantee great results.

By definition, a less volatile fund would usually hold more conservative stocks, which may not perform as well as more aggressive stocks.

Big losses can demolish your portfolio returns mercilessly.

In the final analysis it always comes back to the principle of risk and reward. Greater risks attract greater rewards; lesser risks attract lesser rewards. We'll have more to say about market declines in the next lesson: "Recovery from Market Losses."

Consider This!

Perhaps the best way to protect yourself against big losses is to diversify your portfolio across the three major asset classes of reserves, fixed-income, and equities by using several funds to meet your investment objectives.

This book is based on the notion that you are the CFO of **ME, Inc.** *One of the most successful investors in the institutional money management industry concurs with this way of seeing things. He put it this way. "Why must you learn about investing? You can hire a financial planner or manager to make the decisions, cash your dividend cheques, and try to forget about the whole business. But no matter how much responsibility you delegate, and how much you receive, the fate of your portfolio rests in your hands. Think of it this way: You're the CEO of an important enterprise called, Your Financial Future."*

– Peter Lynch

Recovery from Market Losses

Depending upon the depth of a stock market loss the recovery process can appear to be an insurmountable, if not impossible task, to get an investor's portfolio back on track – the deeper the losses, the steeper the climb. For example, a capital loss of 20% requires a gain of 25% to get back to break even; whereas a loss of 50% would require a gain of 100% to get back to break even.

Capital Gain Required to Break Even From Market Losses				
Investment	$50,000	$50,000	$50,000	$50,000
Capital Loss	$10,000	$15,000	$20,000	$25,000
Capital After Loss	$40,000	$35,000	$30,000	$25,000
Capital Loss %	20%	30%	40%	50%
Capital Gain Required to Break Even %	25%	43%	67%	100%

This latter loss would seem an impossible feat to recover. However some past market recoveries have delivered amazing advances after reaching their bear market lows. In the debt crisis recession of 1981–1982 the market declined 43% from peak to trough and from its lowest point of maximum pessimism in July, 1982 it turned out to be the investor's greatest opportunity advancing 84% within the first year of its recovery. Similarly, the derivative global debt crisis of 2008–2009 declined 49% in about 9 months and from its lowest point regained 58% of its losses within the first year of its recovery.

Past Market Recoveries

Bear Market Begins	Main Event	Duration (Months)	Decline %	Maximum Pessimism/ Opportunity	Growth 1-Year Later
7/17/81	Debt Crisis Recession	11.7	43%	07/08/82	84%
6/17/08	Global Debt Crisis	8.7	49%	09/03/09	58%

Of course, no one knows for sure how long a market cycle will take to play itself out. However, based on market history, we expect that equities will eventually lead the parade to recovery and over the long haul will perform better than the other asset classes.

The deeper the losses, the steeper the climb.

For individuals who are just a few years away from retirement, a severe loss at this stage of the lifecycle can be a traumatic experience often forcing them to reconsider their retirement start date, pension, and/or their investment options. Essentially there are three major options from which to choose:

1. Retire at a lower standard of living than planned
2. Remain in the workforce longer – part time or full time
3. Increase savings and or return on investment.

Generally, most individuals utilize some combination of these options when they are on the doorstep of retirement.

Consider This!

Investors know from experience that even though stocks decline in bear market cycles, if they stay the course they will eventually rebound. For example, when the technology bubble burst during 2000 to 2002, stocks declined on average 49% and then from the lowest point of the bear market in 2002 they rallied back up over 100% by 2007.

To succeed in the market, you must have discipline, flexibility – and patience. You have to wait for the tape to give its message before you buy or sell.

– Martin Zweig

Dividend Reinvestment Plans

Investing all year round can be relatively quick and easy with the help of a Dividend Reinvestment Plan (DRIP), a plan that offers investors a convenient, cost effective way to increase their equity in the company by reinvesting cash dividends issued by the company in additional shares without paying a commission. As well, some companies allow you to purchase additional shares at a slight discount to the market without paying brokerage commissions; this is called a Share Purchase Plan (SPP).

Commission free or cheaper purchases are not the only reasons to belong to a DRIP; rising dividend yield is another. Though the current dividend may be low – say 1% or 2%, that particular company may have increased its dividend steadily over the past years such that the dividend rate has grown by as much as several hundred percent. When reinvested, dividends return dividends themselves; little dividends become big sums when compounded. This technique is referred to as dividend compounding.

There are several dozen quality blue-chip companies that offer DRIPs in Canada. Each of these companies has compiled a history of improved earnings and a sustained record of paying out a portion of their earnings in the form of dividends that they have increased over time. As a result the stock price of these companies tends to go up over time because of the improved earnings. But more importantly, as the dividend per share goes up over time, the original cost base of the shares remains the same, and therefore the running yield continues to rise with each subsequent dividend increase.

How to Establish a DRIP
To sign up for a dividend reinvestment program follow these steps:

- First, make sure the company offers a DRIP.
- Buy at least one share of the company that interests you.
- Contact the transfer agent directly or ask your financial advisor to register you for that company's DRIP. The transfer agent, who keeps a record of shareholders and distributes dividends, will hold any shares you acquire in your name.

- Once you are registered, any dividends issued to you by the company will be automatically reinvested in more stock, usually on a quarterly basis.
- Use the option to buy additional shares for cash, if available.

A Failsafe Strategy to Improve Your Return on Investment

Two of the reasons to invest in the stock market over time are to obtain dividends and capital appreciation. Sophisticated investors look for the opportunity to purchase high-quality stocks at low price earnings multiples, with dividend yields ideally in the 3% to 5% range and higher, in order to build a value-based portfolio that can withstand the test of time. In a declining market, stocks that pay dividends generally have an advantage because they appeal to investors who rely on their dividend cash flow. The type of companies that offer a long-term dividend usually are those that offer products or services that are an integral part of our day-to-day lives and therefore they are in demand and fare much better than non-dividend payers by a substantial margin.

> **In a declining market, stocks that pay dividends generally have an advantage because they appeal to investors who rely on their dividend cash flow.**

Companies usually pay dividends quarterly. It is possible to design a laddered portfolio such that you can receive dividends every month of the year. Companies that pay dividends will follow one of three cycles:

- January, April, July, and October
- February, May, August, and November
- March, June, September, and December

If you want to invest each month during the accumulation phase of your life to enjoy all of the benefits of a DRIP program including the benefits of dollar cost averaging; or if you want to receive dividend income each month during the distribution phase of your life in retirement, it is as simple as building a well balanced portfolio by choosing stocks with different dividend payment cycles. Here is an example:

Drip Stock Examples *	Quarterly Payments		
	Jan/Apr July/Oct	Feb/May Aug/Nov	Mar/Jun Sept/Dec
Telus Corp.	X		
Transalta Corp.	X		
TransCanada Corp.	X		
Bank of Montreal		X	
Brookfield Asset Management		X	
Royal Bank		X	
Enbridge			X
Fortis Inc.			X
Suncor Energy Inc.			X

By following such a simple procedure you would most likely achieve a better average return than 90% of the professionally managed equity mutual funds in Canada. Why? You would have paid no commissions or annual management fees and expenses.

* *The securities listed in this chart example are for illustration purposes only. Under no circumstances should this be construed as an offer to sell or the solicitation of an offer to buy any securities.*

Did You Know?

Procter and Gamble has raised its dividend every year for 52 years in a row. The company's annual report is crystal clear: "Our first discretionary use of cash is dividend payments." Dividend payments come out of free cash flow. Free cash flow determines bonuses for P&G executives, giving them a great incentive to treat shareholders to a growing stream of income.

Consider This!

Payout ratios matter, in fact, the higher the better. A research paper compiled by Arnott and Assness in 2002, studied 130 years of data ending in 2001, and discovered that the higher the dividend payout ratio the faster the company's future earnings grow.

Companies in the first quartile – that paid the highest percentage of their earnings out as dividends – had subsequent 10-year earnings growth averaging 3.2% compounded. The second, third and fourth quartiles had earnings growth averaging 2.1%, 1.3%, and -0.7% respectively.

Be prepared. There is paperwork involved with a large portfolio of DRIPs. However, the time involved in keeping track of your paperwork is more than worth it. Your hours are better spent watching your DRIPs, then in following the market's every twist and turn.

— *Peter Lynch*

Buy and Hold Strategy

Generally, a buy and hold strategy will produce much higher returns than a trading strategy in search of quick profits. Buy and hold is a passive strategy whereby stocks are held for a long time regardless of fluctuations in the market. The theory is to choose good quality companies and as long as they remain good, continue to add to your position for the long term.

One need look no further than the success enjoyed by Warren Buffet with his company, Berkshire Hathaway that has owned securities such as Coca Cola for several decades. In fact, the return on investment has been so good that if the Coca Cola position were sold it would attract a $4 billion tax bill on the capital gains.

John Bogle, chairman and founder of the Vanguard Group which has the largest group of index funds worldwide, has completed a number of studies that point out the perils of market timing and active trading compared with the true benefits of a buy and hold strategy as measured by an index fund.

> **Generally, a buy and hold strategy will produce much higher returns than a trading strategy in search of quick profits.**

When Should a Buy and Hold Strategy be Reviewed?

1. When the price of a stock falls significantly or a mutual fund is underperforming its peer group, ask yourself if you would put new money into it now. If the answer is no, consider selling.

2. When the management changes in a company or a mutual fund manager who has achieved a great track record leaves, you need to assess the abilities of the new manager(s). If within two or three quarters the performance is not measuring up to the past results, consider selling.

3. Most investors expect too much, too soon. Give your portfolio time to perform and be aware of downgrading quality for the lure of a higher yield. Throughout the years quality stocks and mutual funds have proved to be the long-term yield champions based on their total returns from dividends and capital gains.

4. When a company goes through a merger or an acquisition you need to assess the terms of the transaction as to how it will affect the value of your stock position on a go forward basis.

Manage Your Turnover Ratio

Successful investors tend to maintain a lower turnover ratio (TR), typically around 20%. Less successful investors generally have higher turnover ratios from trading more frequently and make less money.

To calculate your TR simply add up the value of the stocks you bought and sold during the course of the year, and divide by two. Then divide your answer by your portfolio's year-end value to determine your TR.

Case Profile: Rachel Bloomfield, age 35, Portfolio Value $106,000
Rachel is an extremely conservative investor with a low tolerance for risk. Her philosophy is to seek out good value stocks that ideally will perform well over several years or more. Last year Rachel's portfolio transactions were as follows:

Stocks Bought	$20,500
Stocks Sold	$14,300
Total Value of Transactions	**$34,800**

Average Value of Transactions (AVT)
$34,800 / 2 = $17,400

Turnover Ratio = AVT/Portfolio Value
$17,400 / $106,000 = 16.4%

Did You Know?

Stocks tend to outperform other investments and also inflation over long time periods. Most investors who jump in and out of the markets inevitably find it is difficult to do so at the right time.

Consider This!

At the end of the day, the most successful investors are not the ones jumping on the latest trends, but the ones who have a well thought-out strategy, who stick to it during good times and bad, and who know what they own and why they own it.

Investors need to avoid the negatives of buying fads, crummy companies, and timing the market. Buying an index fund over a long period of time makes the most sense.

– Warren Buffett

What provides the best chance for investor success is to design a portfolio of asset classes based on one's risk tolerance, and most importantly minimize investment costs and taxes, which are the biggest killer of returns.

– Jack Bogle, Vanguard

Market Timing Strategy

Very few investors are able to beat the markets with any degree of consistency by switching securities within or between asset classes on a regular basis. Even the professional money managers struggle to beat the market indices by a few percentage points from year to year. In fact, most years fewer professional managers beat the market averages than the majority who usually underperform. To some degree this poor performance is caused by excessive management expense ratios (MERs).

Similarly, when an individual investor trades excessively, inevitably the transaction costs are bound to increase which will affect the return on investment (ROI) of the investor's portfolio. Some mutual fund companies allow switches within their family of funds at no cost, although the prospectus often permits fees of up to 2%, which can be charged by one's advisor; other funds charge a flat fee per transaction after a limited number of free switches.

Switches between asset classes can be profitable if an investor can determine the direction of interest rates in the economy. For example, when interest rates decline, bond prices increase based on the inverse relationship between interest rates and price, therefore an equity to bond switch has a good chance of being successful.

> **Very few investors are able to beat the markets with any degree of consistency by switching securities within or between asset classes on a regular basis.**

Switches within the equity asset class are much riskier because you have to guess right on the future performance of two different industries. Past market cycles indicate that various industries perform better at some times than others. Students of the market may be able to predict these cycles and take advantage of buying and/or selling into these market swings. However, it is not as easy as one might think and many fortunes have been lost.

There are significant costs involved with maintaining an active trading posture:

1. There are commission costs incurred every time you buy and sell.
2. The spread between the bid and ask price (the price at which a buyer offers to pay versus the price at which a seller offers a security for sale) can increase your cost significantly.
3. Capital gains are taxed resulting in less capital to invest.
4. Dividend payments will be foregone if you have sold the stock prior to a dividend record date.
5. If your trading strategy fails you'll lose substantial potential profits. No investor has a perfect track record. You would do well to win on 7 out of every 10 trades. The 3 losses out of every 10 trades can decimate your overall return including a substantial loss of capital.

Mutual funds are not designed for short-term trading and unlike individual equities that trade throughout the day. Mutual funds are valued at the end of each day based on the day's closing prices for each of the stocks held within the fund. It is difficult to take advantage of major market investments either up or down. And if you choose to try your hand at short-term trading you would be better off investing directly in a portfolio of individual stocks.

Did You Know?

Many of the corporate-sponsored defined contribution plans monitor the results of plan members' activity within the plan during the year. In almost every case those members who employ market-timing strategies do not perform as well as those who adopt a buy and hold strategy. As a result many group providers have instituted frequent trading fees to curtail excessive trading activity in group programs.

Consider This!

Portfolio Guidelines

One strategy to consider is to design a "core and explore" approach in which most of your money is allocated to a diversified cross-section of mutual funds (core), while a smaller percentage is devoted to specialty or sector funds and/or individual stocks (explore). However, before you embark on any new course of action, be sure to obtain professional advice.

Most investors' time horizons are much too short. Statistics indicate that day trading is largely based on luck.

– Richard Bernstein

The public buys the most at the top and the least at the bottom.

– Jeffrey Saut

Professional Money Management Styles

There are three major types of money management personalities:

- Value investor
- Sector rotator investor
- Growth investor

Make sure your manager's style and personality suit your personality and way of thinking.

Value (Bottom-Up Style) This investor seeks undervalued securities with little regard for overall economic and market conditions, selects stocks trading at a discount to book value and low price-earnings multiple, and is prepared to sit with the selected security for many years in order to recognize the stock's full potential.

Sector Rotator (Top-Down Style) This investor analyzes the macro and micro economic trends and market forecasts, then selects attractive groups to participate in, with stocks that are the leaders and show the most promise in their industry.

Growth (Diversified) This type of investor combines the bottom-up and the top-down style to select a cross-section of securities poised for above-average growth over the intermediate to long term and selects stocks based on fundamentals with above average increases in cash flow, revenues, earnings per share, or market share.

Growth (Balanced Asset Allocation) This type of investor combines the bottom-up and top-down styles and measures risk/reward by mathematical analysis of various classes of common shares, preferred shares, bonds, and debentures, and a variety of money market assets in order to reduce risk. This investor uses fundamental analysis of economic growth, interest rates, and market analysis of securities.

Hedged Style This type of investor can use any of the above approaches individually or together, including derivatives to enhance portfolio performance. A typical strategy that provides a less volatile performance is selling options on securities held in the portfolio. The premiums earned on the options provide steady income, but the hedged style also precludes the possibility of superior capital gains if the underlying stock is called away should the purchaser exercise this option.

Market Timers These investors use technical analysis based on price trends for individual stocks or stock groups or market as a whole. Really good market timers are a rare breed and very hard to find.

In addition to learning as much as you can about the manager's investment philosophy, strategy, and style, look for a verifiable long-term record of performance over one, three, five, and ten years, encompassing both good and bad market periods.

Management Style Equities

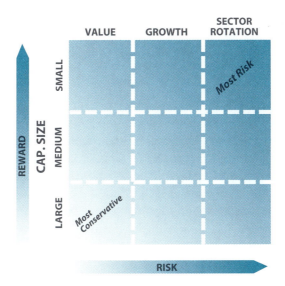

How to Monitor the Performance of Your Money Manager – Canadian Equities

How can you measure the performance of a professional money manger? The Institute recommends using the investment industry's common performance criteria for a complete market cycle of approximately four to five years. If the money manager is performing well, his/her performance over the period of this market cycle will:

1. Exceed the Consumer Price Index by 1% to 3% compounded per year
2. Outperform the S&P/TSX Total Return Index by 2% to 3% compounded per year
3. Perform in the top quartile among his/her peer group of managers
4. Outperform the S&P/TSX Composite Index during all down years.

Management Styles
As we discussed, there are three key management styles – value, growth, and sector rotation. There are other styles such as market timing and momentum investing, but they are not as popular nor are they for the faint of heart. There are also three sizes of stocks often referred to as large cap, mid cap, or small cap. Cap pertains to the capitalization or value of a company. If an investor were to consider the most conservative investment posture of all, it would probably be to invest in the value style with a large capitalization. A value managerial style looks for stocks that trade at very low price earnings multiples, and the value manager is prepared to wait long term for an investment to perform.

If an investor were to invest at the other extreme, which would carry a greater degree of risk, it would be sector rotation with a small capitalization. Sector rotation, just by the name itself, implies a managerial style that is concentrated in only one or two specific industries. This implies higher risk as the portfolio would not be diversified through 10 or 12 different industries or more. A sector rotation manager is betting the farm on one or two industries playing those sectors for all they're worth.

When a portfolio is limited to just a few industries it will carry much higher risk.

What is the "best" style?
Attempting to predict which equity fashions or fads are going to be in vogue at any point in the market cycle is futile for most investors. Therefore many financial professionals suggest that owning a basket of funds embracing all of the styles will smooth out the inevitable ups and downs in the market cycles.

To summarize the various styles:

- Value investors want to own cheap stocks that will eventually rise to reflect their true value.
- Growth investors want to own companies that will continue to grow without disappointment.
- Market timers want to buy and sell in advance of market swings.
- Asset allocators want to heavily weight whatever will produce the best returns.
- Group rotators want to switch from industry to industry in the right sequence.
- And momentum investors want everything to go their way.

Style matters and studies show that the market environment can change from year to year. Typically, different styles will shine, while others fade only to have their moment in the limelight another year. Investors who are uncomfortable with trying to time these style shifts might be well advised to buy and hold a basket of securities or funds embracing two or three styles.

Alternatively, an investor could choose to invest in an index fund that would embrace a multiple of these styles and at a much lower cost than the actively managed styles mentioned above.

Many financial professionals suggest that owning a basket of funds embracing all of the styles will smooth out the inevitable ups and downs in the market cycles.

Did You Know?

U.S. investment superstars Peter Lynch and Warren Buffett are both practitioners of bottom-up investing. They will not buy stock in a company unless they know it really well. Over time a disciplined, smart, bottom-up investor beats the stock market index.

Consider This!

Value versus Growth Style Descriptors

In classifying a management style as value or growth, there is an inherent assumption that the given manager holds to a mechanical and absolute employment of the described style. In other words, a manager employs a value or growth style and "never the twain shall meet."

Growth versus Value
How to assess a Canadian equity manager's style

Portfolio Characteristics	Value Managers vs. S&P/TSX	Growth Managers vs. S&P/TSX
Price-earning ratio	Less	Greater
Dividend yield	Greater	Less
Price-to-book ratio	Less	Greater
Return on equity	Less	Greater
Dividend growth	Less	Greater
Forecasted growth	Less	Greater

Source: Frank Russell Canada Ltd.

If a man empties his purse into his head, no man can take it away from him. An investment in knowledge always pays the best interest.

– Benjamin Franklin

On market timing… October. This is one of the most dangerous months in which to speculate in stocks. Others are: July, January, September, April, November, May, March, June, December, August, and February!

– Mark Twain

SECTION 5
INVESTMENT MANAGEMENT

Advanced Tools & Techniques

Canadian Income Taxes

Most of what we will be discussing in this lesson concerns personal, non-registered investments. It does not apply to employer-sponsored pension plans or personal RRSPs. Canada utilizes a progressive tax system similar to many other countries by collecting taxes from individuals and companies to help pay for government programs and services. In return we receive many benefits that are paid for with our taxes: roads, public utilities, schools, health care, transfer payments, government income security programs such as Old Age Security (OAS) and the Guaranteed Income Supplement (GIS).

Canadians must pay taxes on their world income from all sources including employment income, interest, dividends, capital gains and any other sources. Canadians pay both federal and provincial taxes and combined the rates ranging upwards to 49% for taxpayers in the highest marginal tax bracket.

Good tax planning consists of arranging your financial affairs to achieve your personal objectives at the lowest tax cost. There are two major objectives to consider:

1. How to reduce your taxable income
2. How to reduce your effective tax rate

These objectives can be accomplished using several different tax planning strategies including:

Income splitting – transferring family income from a taxpayer in a higher tax bracket to one in a lower tax bracket. The pension income splitting rules allow spouses to split up to 50% of income received from employer pension plans; registered retirement income funds (RRIFs); annuities and life income funds (LIFs); subject only to age restrictions for some types of pension income.

Income shifting – transferring income from a high tax year to a year when your tax rate will be lower. This event occurs for most people when they retire but it can also occur when changing jobs mid career or when faced with a downsizing or early leave.

Tax deferral – delaying taxation and the payment of taxes until a future date. The purchase of RRSPs is a good example of a tax deferral strategy whereby current contributions receive a tax reduction and receive tax-free compounding and tax deferred status until the funds are withdrawn.

Tax shelters – the use of government approved incentives to minimize taxable income on investments. There have been a number of tax shelters/limited partnerships introduced during the last few decades including multiple unit residential buildings (MURBs); flow-through shares; feature length movies; scientific research and experimental development tax credits; and labour-sponsored investment funds (LSIFs). The vast majority of these tax shelters have proven to be disastrous investments. While the investors in each case would have received an incentive to save paying some taxes, the underlying investments have rarely done well. In fact, many are worth absolutely nothing.

Investment income – choosing your investments so as to take advantage of tax exemptions or credits on investment income. There are three basic forms of investment income: interest, dividends, and capital gains. Each type of income is treated differently for tax purposes. Therefore, it is more important for an investor to focus on an investment's after-tax return than on its pre-tax return.

Good tax planning consists of arranging your financial affairs to achieve your personal objectives at the lowest tax cost. There are two major objectives to consider:

1. **How to reduce your taxable income**
2. **How to reduce your effective tax rate**

Interest Dividends and Capital Gains – After-tax Comparisons

Interest income does not receive any special tax treatment and is fully taxed just like your employment income. Interest income must be reported annually in the year the interest is received or earned.

Dividends received from Canadian corporations are eligible for a dividend tax credit. The amount of the credit depends on the type of corporation paying the dividend. Most dividends received from

Canadian public corporations are eligible for the enhanced dividend tax credit (eligible dividends), while most dividends received from Canadian controlled private corporations (CCPCs) are eligible for the regular or small business dividend tax credit. The chart below illustrates the tax treatment for dividends received from Canadian public corporations.

Capital gains on the sale of an asset will occur if the asset is sold for a greater sum than its adjusted cost base (ACB). Similarly, a capital loss will occur if the asset is sold for less than its ACB. To determine your taxable capital gain (loss), each asset that is sold (less costs associated with the sale) is taxable on 50% of the gain/loss.

Case Profile: Diane Summers
Combined Federal/Provincial (Average) Marginal Tax Rate of 33% on Income of $65,000

Description	Interest	Dividends	Capital Gains
Taxable Income	$1,000	$1,000	$1,000
Marginal Tax Rate – 33%	$330	$86	$165
Net Income	$670	$914	$835

In the case profile for Diane Summers her marginal tax rate is 33% on her income of $65,000 per year. Looking at the tax treatment on $1000 of various types of income we learn the following:

- *The interest income is fully taxed at her marginal rate of 33% therefore the tax department will get $330 and Diane will be left with $670.*
- *The dividend income from a Canadian public corporation after accounting for the dividend tax credit will incur a net tax of $86 and Diane will get to keep $914.*
- *The capital gain of $1000 is only taxable on 50% of the gain, therefore $500 taxed at her marginal tax rate of 33% will incur taxes of $165 and Diane will have net income totaling $835.*

As you can see Diane gets to keep much more income from dividends and capital gains than she does from interest, and her dividends and capital gains usually come from the same source – ownership of common shares of Canadian public corporations.

In the case profile that follows for Maria Zajac, her marginal tax rate is 46% on income of $150,000 per year. While she is in a substantially higher tax bracket then Diane Summers she also gets to keep much more of her income from dividends and capital gains than she does from interest.

Case Profile: Maria Zajac
Combined Federal/Provincial (Average) Marginal Tax Rate of 46% on Income of $150,000

Description	Interest	Dividends	Capital Gains
Taxable Income	$1,000	$1,000	$1,000
Marginal Tax Rate – 46%	$464	$246	$232
Net Income	$536	$754	$768

Consider This!

You cannot help the poor by destroying the rich.

You cannot establish sound security on borrowed money.

You cannot keep out of trouble by spending more than you earn.

You cannot help men permanently by doing for them what they could and should do for themselves.

– **Abraham Lincoln**

It's the duty of a good Shepherd to sheer his sheep, but not to skin them.

– *Tiberius Caesar*

If you get up early, work late, and pay your taxes, you will get ahead – if you strike oil.

– *J. Paul Getty*

Nothing in this world is certain but death and taxes.

– *Benjamin Franklin*

Taxflation

Now that we've looked at marginal tax brackets and inflation you can use the following table to estimate your personal break-even rate of return. The table shows the rate of return on investments you would need to obtain to break even at various levels of income tax and inflation. First, find your marginal tax rate on the vertical axis and circle it. Second, find the rate of inflation you anticipate on the horizontal axis. The percentage shown where these two lines intersect is your break-even rate of return.

Break-even Rate on Taxes and Inflation

Tax Bracket	Inflation Rate (%)					
	3%	4%	5%	6%	7%	8%
25%	4.0	5.3	6.6	8.0	9.3	10.7
30%	4.3	5.7	7.1	8.6	10.1	11.4
35%	4.6	6.2	7.7	9.2	10.8	12.3
40%	5.0	6.6	8.3	10.0	11.7	13.3
45%	5.5	7.2	9.1	10.9	12.7	14.5
50%	6.0	8.0	10.0	12.0	14.0	16.0

Case Profile: Sergio Di Palma, age 39, income $67,000
Sergio has a combined federal/provincial marginal tax rate of 34% on income of $67,000. From the chart he selects the marginal tax rate closest to his personal situation or 35%, and he assumes the long-term inflation rate will average 4%. He discovers he will need to generate a 6.2% return on his taxable investments just to break even!

Think in terms of a total portfolio positioned efficiently at the proper time to beat inflation. Your assets should be allocated to maximize your after-tax return, balanced against a level of risk that provides you with peace of mind.

Personal Portfolio Allocation

This exercise has given Sergio an incredible wake-up call.

He has been maintaining an asset allocation of fixed income (bonds) 40% and equities 60% in his portfolio for the past several years that has been generating the following returns:

Description	Portfolio Asset Allocation		Rate of Return	
Bonds	40%	x	6.6%	2.64%
Equities	60%	x	8.0%	4.80%
Average Rate of Return				7.44%
Less Sergio's Break-even Rate of Return				6.20%
Sergio's Net Rate of Return				1.24%

Sergio was shocked to discover that he was earning just over a 1% net return on his personal investments.

Employer-Sponsored Pension Plan

Sergio then decided to review his employers defined contribution pension plan. This exercise enabled him to appreciate the value of the immediate tax reduction benefit he obtained with each contribution, the benefit from years of tax-free compounding, and the fact that his pension assets would be tax deferred until removed during his retirement.

Description	Portfolio Asset Allocation		Rate of Return	
Bonds	30%	x	7.1%	2.10%
Equities	70%	x	8.6%	6.02%
Average Rate of Return				8.12%
Less Assumed Rate of Inflation 4% and Tax Bracket 25% at Retirement				5.30%
Sergio's Net Rate of Return				2.82%

Sergio realized the additional 1.58% rate of return he was earning in his company-sponsored pension plan was due to the professional *management of the investments and the economies of scale afforded to a large pension plan for management fees and expenses. It became very clear to Sergio just how valuable his pension plan was in helping him accumulate money for his retirement.*

Earlier we learned that there are only two ways to increase your real wealth (defined as your net rate of return after taxes and inflation) and both ways require ownership investments in equities and/or real estate. Because of the special treatment of Canadian dividend income and capital gains – ownership investments provide dual benefits in offsetting the ravages of taxes and inflation.

Think in terms of a total portfolio positioned efficiently at the proper time to beat inflation. Your assets should be allocated to maximize your after-tax return, balanced against a level of risk that provides you with peace of mind.

Did You Know?

Over 50% of car buyers lease their vehicles often at rates of 3.9%, 5.9%, and higher depending on the level of interest rates in the economy. Car loans are often in the $20,000 to $40,000 range.

Assume you lease 10 cars for 4 years each over a working lifetime of 40 years, what would your interest costs be on an average loan of $25,000 outstanding over those 40 years at a rate of 6% Answer: $48,620.

Now let's further assume you had $25,000 to invest for 40 years at 6% per year compounded annually, what would be the lost opportunity cost? Answer: $257,143.

The underlying message here is that an individual can spend a lot of money for interest payments on a depreciating asset over a lifetime. Therefore, if an individual would purchase only as much vehicle as he or she could afford to drive, and instead invest a one-time cost of a vehicle at $25,000 for 40 years at 6% the result would be over one quarter million dollars of additional capital to supplement your retirement.

Consider This!

Question: What is the most important financial planning question all individuals must ask themselves?

Answer: Will your current asset allocation strategies provide the purchasing power you'll need for your retirement?

There's a lot of evidence you can sell people on tax increases if they think it's an investment.

– Bill Clinton

Should I Pay Down My Mortgage, Top Up My RRSP, or Start Up a TFSA?

One of the biggest questions of financial planning is whether to invest for the future in an RRSP or reduce debt by paying down the mortgage.

First, let's look at how the tax act treats your home, RRSP, and TFSA.

Tax Treatment	Principal Residence	RRSP	TFSA
How is money paid in treated?	After-tax dollars	Deductible from taxable income.	After-tax dollars
Is there a dollar limit?	No dollar limit	Yes, up to $22,000 or 18% of earned income in 2010.	Yes. Maximum in 2009 is $5,000; 2010 is $5,000; 2011 is $5,000.
Is there a maximum age limit?	No	Yes. Must convert at age 71.	No
How is investment growth treated?	Not taxed at all	Not taxed as long as it is not paid out.	Not taxed at all
How is money paid out treated?	Tax-free	Added to your taxable income	Tax-free

The new TFSA is taxed the same way as your principal residence: you don't get a tax break on the money you put in, but the value created will never be taxed.

How Do the Investment Characteristics Compare?

Real estate is not very liquid. Buying a house takes a bit of time and is purchased for many reasons besides investment considerations. Getting into an RRSP or TFSA does not involve a large upfront amount of money. It only takes a quick trip to the bank for some forms to sign up for regular contributions. Withdrawing money from an RRSP or TFSA may involve fees and penalties, but you can usually get at your money in a few days. To get at the money invested in your home can mean selling the property or borrowing against it. Nowadays, most mortgage lenders are happy to arrange a home equity line of credit that makes cash as accessible as your bank account or credit card.

Diversification
There's a broad range of different investments that qualify for RRSPs and TFSAs, so you can easily diversify your portfolio. However, by definition, you only have one principal residence, so the money invested in your home is not diversified. Of course, having a chunk of your money in real estate diversifies your holdings away from purely financial assets!

Fees
Most investments held in RRSPs and TFSAs involve fees – explicit or implicit. For example, the average annual MER for an equity mutual fund is in the 2% to 3% range. There are also costs when purchasing a home and setting up a mortgage. However, once the home is purchased, the expenses associated with maintaining it are mostly taxes and maintenance. Other ongoing costs such as heating, hydro, and home insurance apply whether you rent or own, so they should not be considered costs of the investment: you'd have to pay them anyway.

Simplicity and Transparency
Compared with many of the new and sophisticated "derivative" and "alternative" investments available in the global financial markets, home ownership is easy to understand. It is tangible and local: we can see with our own eyes what determines the value of a property and how it can change over time.

Unique Advantages
You live in your home. You can't live inside an RRSP or a TFSA. You can improve your home's value directly by doing renovations. Try that with a mutual fund or a GIC inside your RRSP or TFSA!

And, finally, you don't have to sell it to enjoy it.

> **The new TFSA is taxed the same way as your principal residence; you don't get a tax break on the money you put in, but the value created will never be taxed.**

Did You Know?

You can designate a property as your principal residence if it meets all of the following conditions:

- It is a housing unit, a leasehold interest in a housing unit, or a share of the capital stock of a co-operative housing corporation you acquire, only to get the right to inhabit a housing unit owned by that corporation.
- You own the property alone or jointly with another person.
- You, your current or former spouse or common-law partner, or any of your children live in it.

Usually, the amount of land that you can consider as part of your principal residence is limited to 1/2 hectare (5,000 square metres), or about 1.24 acres (53,819 square feet).

Happiness is a government that lives within its income and without mine.

– Unknown

You've all heard about the Canada Revenue Agency two-step whereby they giveth with the right hand and taketh with the left. They just constantly waltz you around.

– Unknown

Make Market Sentiment Work for ME, Inc.

Market sentiment is one of the most reliable guides in the measurement of investor optimism or pessimism at each stage of a market cycle. The two major drivers that determine the market's direction are fear and greed. When investors express too much fear, markets often overreact and stocks are underpriced on the downside; too much greed and stocks become overbought on the upside.

Market folklore states that the stock market is an expensive place to learn how to invest. Most investors are not good traders because they allow their emotions to overrule logic. Quite simply, when it comes to common stock buy and sell decisions, "you got to know when to hold'em and know when to fold'em."

Sentiment Indicators

To become a more successful investor you need to learn about a few time-tested sentiment indicators to help you navigate your **ME, Inc**. portfolio to positive results. What are some of these indicators?

The Trend is Your Friend – This indicator is based on the number of stocks advancing versus declining; and the number of new highs versus new lows. Thomas Dorsey, in his book, *Point and Figure Charting*, states that the overall direction of the market has a 66% influence on the overall movement of an individual stock. In other words an individual stock is more likely to go up in price if the whole market is advancing or vice versa.

The Highs/Lows (H/L) line is a market breadth indicator that compares the number of stocks on an index that are making new 52-week highs with the number of stocks making new 52 week lows and thus indicating whether the overall market is in a bullish or bearish trend. When more stocks are reaching new 52-week highs than are reaching new 52-week lows the H/L line moves higher and therefore the bullish sentiment in the market is increasing. Similarly when more stocks are reaching new 52-week lows than are reaching new 52-week highs the H/L line moves lower and therefore the bearish sentiment in the market is increasing.

Advisory Newsletter Services – There are literally hundreds of newsletter services (both print and electronic media) that provide information and advice on many market-related topics and individual securities. In the US there is a weekly poll of stock newsletter writers called the Investors Intelligence Survey. This survey has an amazing track record of gauging investor sentiment. The index is based on contrarian opinion whereby it is assumed that the consensus opinion is usually wrong and investors should act opposite to the majority opinion. Whenever the balance of opinion is skewed strongly in one direction a reversal is usually forthcoming thus presenting an opportunity for an investor to take advantage of the market's change in direction.

News Magazine Headlines – are another contrarian sentiment indicator that often provides a signal when markets are about to reverse their direction. As with the newsletter services the major business publications often provide bullish headlines and pictures on their covers when the markets are about to decline, and bearish headlines right at the time when the markets are about to recover.

> **Most investors are not good traders because they allow their emotions to overrule logic.**

The Psychology of Crowds – This indicator, at its most fundamental level and driven by greed, can cause normally rational individuals to throw caution to the winds and be caught up by the herd instinct, to execute irrational behavior in the acquisition of any commodity. Charles McKay in his book *Extraordinary Popular Delusions and the Madness of Crowds* illustrated this madness regarding the acquisition of tulips in Holland in the 1630s; Tulipmania was followed by the South Sea bubble with real estate in South America in the 1720s; and the stock market crash in United States in 1929 as well as dozens of lesser known bubbles throughout the centuries. In each case there was a bull market in a commodity whereby the investing public believed it would continue forever to the upside.

More recent examples of these mania extremes would be the technology bubble and subsequent burst into the early 2000s, and the more recent real estate bubble and subsequent sub-prime meltdown that began the debt crisis in the latter 2000s experienced by the US, UK, and many other countries. In each case, investors believed that the trend would last forever and so they overextended themselves with debt, in the belief that the technology stocks and real estate they acquired could only ever increase in value.

Every mania in its initial stages is fueled by greed but eventually investor's fears take over and the market collapses on itself when the public panics and attempts to sell only to discover that demand is now non-existent.

Did You Know?

Market moves are caused by shifts in mass psychology — "the herd instinct," economic and world events vying for the investor's consideration.

Investor's behaviour is dictated by an endless battle between optimism and pessimism, fear and greed, and plays out in a series of rhythmic wave patterns in both bull and bear markets.

Most bear markets do not experience panic selling — rather investors enter a state of inertia or inactivity and become merely paralyzed by the market slump.

Unfortunately, most investors are afraid to commit more money during a bear market and inevitably miss incredible opportunities.

Be brave when others are afraid, and be afraid when others are brave.
— **Warren Buffett**

When everyone thinks alike, everyone is likely to be wrong.
— **Humphrey Neill, The Art of Contrary Thinking**

Understand Behavioural Finance to Improve Performance

In both bear (declining) markets and bull (advancing) markets, investor emotions are the strongest driver of investor behaviour. And the most important skill an investor needs to learn is how to manage expectations in the market under any condition, by embracing a balanced view of risk versus return. Every novice investor should complete a risk tolerance profile before they begin to invest in the markets and even seasoned investors may want to review their objectives and risk tolerance at different stages of the life cycle.

Most investors find it much easier to make buy decisions rather than sell decisions in their portfolio, especially if it means selling a security at a loss. However, the most successful investors are those who are most disciplined about culling their losers. And they waste no time about it. Generally, if their analysis shows that some investments should be sold or upgraded in their portfolio, they don't hesitate, because improvements delayed are benefit opportunities delayed.

The most successful investors are those who are most disciplined about culling their losers.

In recent years a new field of behavioural finance has evolved that combines behavioural and psychological theories with conventional economics and finance that provides explanations for why investors make irrational investment decisions. Suffice it to say behavioural finance has made us aware of the many psychological pitfalls that affect investors.

Overconfident – when investors take excessive risk trying to recoup recent losses in the belief that they can outperform the market.

Loss aversion – when an investor is content with low returning investments year after year because of the fear of loss.

Anchoring – when investors anchor themselves to the value of the stock market at some value in the past. For instance does the S&P/TSX at 12,000 feel high or low? Most investors would answer by comparing the figure to where the market traded in the recent past.

For example, an investor who sold out of the market at the 8,000 level would be hard to convince that buying at the 12,000 level would represent good value, when in fact a number of fundamental ratios and the overall economy might indicate that the market at 12,000 is good value.

Conflicted – a nervous investor who fears market risk but is also motivated by the potential for market rewards, jumps in and out trying to time the market and inevitably loses capital.

Hindsight bias – when investors believe that adverse markets are lurking just around the corner thus preventing them from taking action to participate in an advancing bull market.

Disillusioned – when an investor uses recent market losses as proof that financial markets cannot deliver the results that other asset classes can (such as stocks versus real estate).

Rules for Successful Investing
1. Know thyself! Are you an investor or a speculator? An investor invests money or capital for income or profit. A speculator enters into a transaction or venture; any profits are subject to chance.
2. Understand your risk tolerance and decide on an appropriate balance between safety, liquidity, income, and growth.
3. If the fundamentals are right do not be discouraged by erratic short-term performance. Investing is a long-term marathon, not a short-term 100-metre dash.
4. Dollar-cost averaging is accomplished by making regular periodic capital contributions and is one of the best wealth accumulating strategies.
5. The number one factor that determines the value of equity prices over the long run is earnings growth.
6. A buy and hold philosophy makes sense for most investors who neither have the time nor inclination to trade more actively.
7. Know when to hold'em and when to fold'em. The professional's edge over the amateur when investing is not in guessing the future, but in being able to calculate and measure risk.

Consider This!

Investment Value

Certain products will sell even in the worst bear markets: coca cola, coffee, alcohol, food staples, and so on.

Investors search for value and value is born out of the chaos of bear markets.

Bear markets create the opportunity for sophisticated investors to acquire value stocks that disenheartened people are discarding at bargain basement prices.

This area of enquiry is sometimes referred to as "behavioural finance," but we call it "behavioural economics." Behavioural economics combines the twin disciplines of psychology and economics to explain why and how people make seemingly irrational or illogical decisions when they spend, invest, save, and borrow money.

– Gary Belsky & Thomas Gilovich, Why Smart People Make Big Money Mistakes – and How to Correct Them

In the short run, the stock market is a voting machine. But in the long run, it's a weighing machine.

– Benjamin Graham

Investment Market Forces

The force of the market involves three key areas:

1. **Fundamentals:** sales and revenues, earnings per share, dividends, return on investment, and selectivity
2. **Technical**: economy, industry position, historical data, and chart analysis
3. **Investor Psychology:** confidence, emotion, and the herd instinct.

In addition to the economic law of supply and demand and the changing value of the dollar (important to foreign investors), you need to understand that the stock market is a continuous cycle of peaks and troughs, mostly influenced by investor psychology regarding the current market level in the cycle at any point in time.

Everything in life involves a cycle, beginning with life itself. The reproduction cycle passes from generation to generation. The moon revolves around the earth and contributes to the tides. The earth and moon, together, revolve around the sun, giving us seasons. The earth spins on its axis, giving us day and night. The stock market runs on cycles as well. There is a business cycle, an economic cycle, a presidential election cycle, a goods and services cycle, and a retail marketing cycle, to name a few. All of these cycles cause the stock market to fluctuate.

Everything in life involves a cycle, beginning with life itself.

More zeal and energy, more fanatical hope and more intense anguish have been extended over the past century in efforts to forecast the stock market than in almost any other single line of human action. Adam Smith, in The Money Game, stated, "You have to know what time of market it is".

Investor Psychology at Market Bottom
Investor psychology is usually very negative at or near market bottoms and nervous investors continue to sell stocks and redeem funds in the midst of conflicting media reports such as:

- Uncertainty about the economy and the pace of recovery.
- Analysts/economists are often in two camps: one group is bullish, and sees opportunity; the other group is bearish preaching doom and gloom and suggests the worst is yet to come – recession – depression – deflation!
- Uncertainty is always a part of the investment process. At market bottoms investors are most often confused and bewildered and they allow inertia and apathy to take command of their decision-making capabilities, which results most often in doing absolutely nothing. Exactly the wrong thing to do at market bottoms!

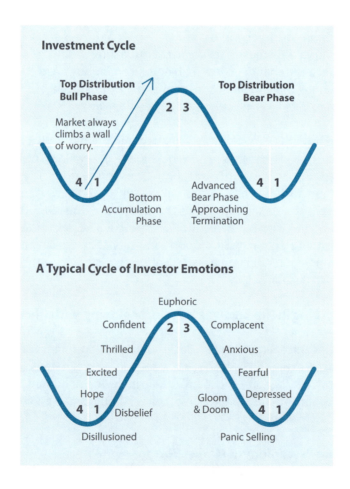

Did You Know?

Investing is an art, not a science.

Successful investors are people who understand the cycles and psychology of the investment marketplace.

Consider This!

In Chinese, the word crisis is composed of two characters, the symbols of danger and opportunity.

CRISIS

A time of change.

A time of opportunity.

In this business if you're good, you're right six or seven times out of ten. You're never going to be right nine times out of ten.

– Peter Lynch

Two Invaluable Concepts to Enhance Investment Returns

1. The Odds Always Favour the House

Historically, the stock market ratio of up/down days has been to increase 70%; decrease 30% of the time. However of all of the thousands of equities that trade on any given day – some move up while others move down but on average over the long term the Canadian stock market (S&P/TSX) has averaged a 10% return.

With the proliferation of new products in the stock market today investors can choose to buy long (if they believe the market is going to advance) or sell short (if they believe it is about to decline). However the house odds over the long term favour the investors who buy long. Why? Investors who sell short are not unlike gamblers who bet on sporting events. Consider the odds each time they bet $100 with their bookmaker. If they win they collect $100; if they lose they have to pay the bookmaker $110 ($100 for the losing bet and a $10 fee for the bookmaker; fees are only paid on losing bets). Therefore in order to break even the bettor has to be right 55% of the time.

The house odds over the long term favour the investors who buy long.

You can deduce from this scenario, investors who are constantly on the short side of the market, would have to be correct more often than not to offset the house odds of 10%, which are stacked against them. Even average stock pickers will lose 10% over the long term because of the unfavourable odds. Conversely mediocre stock pickers or investors who simply rely on index funds could achieve a 10% long-term annual return virtually risk-free based on the long-term performance of the equity markets. The underlying message unless you are a professional investor is to favour the long side of the market.

2. Insider Trading

No one is closer to the day-to-day operations of a company then the people who manage the business. And based on their buy/sell behaviour with respect to their company stock, this will often provide an investor with insight as to the markets likely direction (up or down) with respect to the company's fortunes over the near term.

When management, representing many companies across a range of industries, are net buyers rather than sellers of their companies stocks that would indicate that their sentiment is positive and stronger stock prices could be forthcoming. Conversely, when there are more sellers than buyers the evidence would suggest management's negative mood could lead to the likelihood of declining stock prices.

We assume the view that no one ever sells a stock they believe is going up and that no one knows a company better than its management team (insiders) as to what's really going on in their companies. And therefore, if they are selling rather than buying into the strength of a bear market rally that would give investors a pretty invaluable insight as to the downward direction they believe the market is heading to next.

Consider This!

Two Types of Risk

Pure Risk
Where there is a chance of loss only – e.g., a personal injury whereby a person loses one year of wages. Even if the individual had income disability insurance the wages lost would only be partially covered.

Speculative Risk
Where there is both a chance of gain and loss – e.g., an investor buys a stock that could potentially go either up or down.

Gambling with cards or dice or stocks is all one thing. It's getting money without giving an equivalent for it.

– Henry Ward Beecher

Most of the time common stocks are subject to irrational and excessive price fluctuations in both directions as the consequence of the ingrained tendency of most people to speculate or gamble... to give way to hope, fear, and greed.

– Benjamin Graham

The average man doesn't wish to be told that it is a bull or bear market. What he desires is to be told specifically which particular stock to buy or sell. He wants to get something for nothing. He does not wish to work. He doesn't even wish to have to think.

– Jesse Livermore

Investor Psychology

There is nothing like hands-on practical experience when coping with severe market corrections. No amount of theory can prepare you for a bear market such as 1981–1982 when the market dropped 43% over 12 months, or of the violent waterfall (climax selling) or spike bear market in 1987 when the market dropped 31% in two months, or the technology bubble burst that lasted over two years with a decline of 49% from peak to trough during 2000–2002, or the second greatest bear market in the last century – the Great Recession of 2008–2009 when the market declined 49% in less than 9 months.

It's a very humbling experience to ride this kind of roller coaster but you gain a lot of wisdom from each bear market cycle. The major benefit is to know with absolute certainty that after each bear market cycle eventually there will always emerge a new bull market. In fact, the decade following the 1987 bear market produced gains of almost 500% for those investors who had the courage to stay the course.

Build a Rest of Your Life Plan
In the Institute's workshops we teach a philosophy of investing based on a "rest of your life plan" and it goes something like this. As a whole, Canadians are living longer and attempting to retire earlier. Assuming you retire at age 60 and you expect to live to age 90 the question is, "How much will you need to fund your retirement?" Quite simply, you will most likely need to maintain a well-diversified portfolio with the potential for real growth (after taxes and inflation) to help fund your retirement. During a retirement span of 30 years you could witness several bull and bear markets. And if you are investing for a "rest of your life" plan you may want to consider welcoming the declines as an opportunity to increase your equity exposure to take advantage of the next bull market advance. After all, if you have not done all of your buying yet, why would you want the market to go anywhere but down, so that you have the opportunity to buy more equities when prices are low?

In summary, bull and bear markets don't stop when we retire. What's important is how to determine where you are in the life cycle as it pertains to the market cycle and whether you are a net buyer or net seller of equities. The point, of course, is that a seller's market (bull) is good news if you are taking income from your assets (selling); a buyer's market (bear) is good news if you are accumulating your fortune (buying).

> **The decade following the 1987 bear market produced gains of almost 500% for those investors who had the courage to stay the course.**

Major sell offs such as the 777.68 drop by the Dow Jones Industrial Average (DJIA) on October 19, 1987, are very unnerving for even the most optimistic of investors. How serious was this decline? It ranks first out of all of the large declines in the US market since 1901. The good news is that every decline was followed by substantial market advances within the next six months to two years.

Calm Surrender
During recessionary times it is wise for investors to apply the 3Ss of calm surrender – silence, solitude, and stillness – thereby creating a sanctuary, a safe place, to regroup and rethink their next steps to recovery. Many investors are grieving; and some have beaten themselves up beyond belief. To each of them we suggest it is imperative to embrace a new strategy. The past is past – nothing can change what has already taken place. The only viable strategy going forward is to forget about your market losses to date and focus on what you should do next to create a better financial future.

This may seem a bit harsh for some investors, but there is really no other way to confront any market recession. It is a time to use good old-fashioned common sense rather than emotions – a time to decide with your head – not with your heart! It takes time to move through any bear market recession and we'll only know where the bottom is after we have moved well past it.

The good news is that historically, many of the greatest market fortunes that were made have been made from the depths of bear market recessions. At the risk of sounding uncaring or lacking compassion, we suggest you to take a moment to engage in the following process before we consider the many strategies that will set you back on a course to financial freedom.

Consider This!

Many investors believe they know what the future holds – that they have the knowledge and the smarts to predict stock market performance. Over time they are humbled because markets are not predictable on a consistent basis. Every successful investor eventually learns that being wrong is part of the investment process.

No matter how low a market cycle will decline, eventually good things happen to cheap assets.

When you lose, don't lose the lesson! There is no such thing as failure, rather only the opportunity for a new lesson learned.

Security is mostly a superstition. It does not exist in nature, nor do the children of men as a whole experience it. Avoiding danger is no safer in the long run than outright exposure. Life is either a daring adventure or nothing.

– Helen Keller

Take a moment to breathe deeply and count your many blessings! Your life is so much more than money, especially if you have your physical health balanced with emotional and spiritual wellness. And if you have the love of family including relationships with close friends—you are truly wealthy!

– The Financial Education Insitute of Canada

Most of the time common stocks are subject to irrational and excessive price fluctuations in both directions as the consequence of the ingrained tendency of most people to speculate or gamble – to give way to hope, fear and greed.

– Benjamin Graham

A Long-Term History of Market Cycles

The 2008–2009 bear market dashed the hopes and dreams of millions of investors as they watched their retirement plans disintegrate – many were devastated by losses of 40% or more. Our message to those investors is, "Have courage, we've been here before." In fact during the last century we've had five major declines of a magnitude of 46% or more, and those investors who experienced any one or more of these would tell you that as negative as the outlook is at the bottom of each bear cycle – the market always recovers, given time.

Five Worst DJIA Bear Markets Last 100 Years

Year	Decline	Reason for Decline
1906–1907	49%	US was within one day of becoming insolvent; no central bank; federal bank created in 1913.
1929–1932	89%	Speculative run-up in prices late 1920s. President Hoover increased taxes and cut money supply; in retrospect he should have done the reverse as it drove the country into the worst depression of the century.
1937–1938	51%	Depression had a few big recovery years from the lows of 1932 and got ahead of itself – capital spending and industrial production declined severely and unemployment stood at 20%.
1973–1974	46%	Lingering effects of Vietnam War; Arab oil embargo – oil prices tripled; US pulls the dollar off the gold standard – currency plunges and inflation soars; and Watergate leads to President Nixon's resignation.
2000–2002	50%	Technology bubble in the communications sector and the dot.com craze created frenzied buying of Internet stocks. The bubble burst when capital markets stopped lending for speculative ventures and major corporations cut back on spending budgets. The terrorist's attacks of 9/11 and the corporate accounting scandals in 2001–2002 prolonged the bear market into a third declining year.
2008–2009	53%	Derivative driven credit bubble fuelled a debt laden global financial crisis causing the longest and deepest contraction since the Great Depression. World currencies were under attack while central banks employ massive stimulus (quantitative easing) in an attempt to jump-start their economies and to stabilize their respective banking systems. Chronic high unemployment and real estate prices collapsed in many countries. Canada was an exception as real estate prices increased through that period.

Manic, Euphoric, and Financial Crashes

Thus far we have discussed the ebb and flow of a typical bull/bear market cycle but history is replete with examples of another type of cycle – speculative mania that leads to boom, then bust. Each one of the following bubbles were driven by greed, insanity, and speculative euphoria only to eventually be consumed by fear, panic, and the horror of financial annihilation.

Tulip Bulb Mania – introduced to the Dutch by Turkey in the 1630s wealthy collectors created the speculative mania that eventually caught many Dutch citizens in the bubble. Some people actually mortgaged their homes to pay the price of a single tulip bulb, which had soared from pennies to thousands of florins. By 1637, the Dutch finally recognized that prices had grown to unsustainable heights whereby prices plunged rapidly and thousands of people were financially ruined.

Mississippi Bubble 1718–1720 – John Law, a Scottish financier formed a French company to develop the Mississippi Valley in America by floating shares to exploit the wealth of the French colony. Demand exceeded supply and speculation drove the shares to 50 times their original value. When the dreams of the overstated wealth of the colony were dashed, the shares nose-dived and fortunes were lost.

The Crash of 1929 – The 1920s was a great time of confidence after World War I and the mood of the populace was to acquire wealth. The speculative frenzy to acquire stocks for many citizens was built by borrowing money and leveraging assets to buy more assets. Many of the underlying investments were questionable, for example phantom corporations with no real solid assets. After many years of prosperity and speculative excess a selling panic began in 1929 and the stock market collapsed, triggering the Great Depression of the 1930s.

The Great Depression – 1929–1932 To take yourself back to North America in the late 1920s, you would need to imagine a world quite unlike what we have today. Much of what we take for granted today was absent then.

Families were larger and most depended on a single wage earner. The government's role in the economy was much smaller than today.

The social safety net was rather weak with no employment insurance for workers and no federal deposit insurance for money in the bank. There was no Bank of Canada to control the money supply. No Medicare. No Canada or Quebec Pension Plan and no RRSPs.

There was no free-trade agreement to protect Canadian access to the US market and international trade was subject to the whims of protectionism. Many countries were valuing their currency based on their gold reserves – the Gold Standard, which meant that foreign exchange rates did not float with trade and the supply and demand of currencies.

> **During 2008–2009 – millions of investors watched their portfolios decline by 40% or more. Our message to those investors is, "Have courage, we've been here before."**

Prior to 1929, the stock market had been on a sustained bull run and many fortunes had been made. From 1921 to the autumn of 1929, the level of stock prices increased more than three times. Buying on margin was popular and many ordinary people joined speculators to invest borrowed money in an attempt to get rich quick. As with any boom and bust pattern, storm clouds were gathering and the cycle was destined to play its self out.

On October 24th, 1929, over 12 million shares changed hands on the New York Stock Exchange and the Dow-Jones closed down 11%. The market had hit "Black Thursday". A few days later it was "Black Monday" when the market fell 12.8% and the next day, "Black Tuesday", the market crashed another 11.7% as over 16 million shares were traded.

The peak of 381.17 achieved on September 3rd was a receding milestone as the market touched its low of the year of 198.69 – a drop of over 47% in barely two and a half months.

Was it all about the Stock Market Crash?
Although it is natural to focus on the drama of the stock market, the US money supply was already shrinking and its economic growth had peaked in August of that year. The economic decline bottomed out in March of 1933 after contracting 30.5%. By then, consumer prices had fallen by 24.4% and the US unemployment rate had climbed

to 24.9%. Unemployment stayed in double digits until World War II. One measure of the economic distress was seen in the banking sector. Between 1929 and 1933, out of 24,970 commercial banks in the US, 10,763 failed.

Governments responded to the crisis with multiple interventions, many of which stand as a legacy today. The Depression brought about the creation of federal deposit insurance in the US in 1933, as well as unemployment insurance in 1935.

In Canada, an attempt in 1935 to implement federal unemployment insurance was ruled unconstitutional as it was judged to infringe on provincial jurisdiction. After a constitutional amendment, the Unemployment Insurance Act was finally passed in 1940.

The Depression also prompted the creation of the Bank of Canada in 1934 "to regulate credit and currency in the best interests of the economic life of the nation."

To conclude, let's remember July 8, 1932. With only 720,000 shares traded on the NYSE, that's the day of maximum pessimism and the end point of the market crash that started 33 months earlier. The market was up over 143% 18 months later.

Did You Know?

Super Maximum Investment Opportunities

- Declines of the magnitude 46% or more occur very infrequently

- Most investors will normally only get one or two buying opportunities like this in their lifetime

- The late 2002 market following the technology bubble burst was one of those rare investment opportunities.

A simple rule dictates my buying: Be fearful when others are greedy, and be greedy when others are fearful. And most certainly, fear is now widespread, gripping even seasoned investors. To be sure, investors are right to be wary of highly leveraged entities or businesses in weak competitive positions. But fears regarding the long-term prosperity of the nation's many sound companies make no sense. These businesses will indeed suffer earnings hiccups, as they always have. But most major companies will be setting new profit records 5, 10, 20 years from now.

– Warren Buffett

To make money, you will have to take risk, even if it's just your time on the line. The key to risk taking is knowledge.

– Stuart Wilde

A market is the combined behaviour of thousands of people responding to information, misinformation, and whim.

– Kenneth Chang

Investment Market Cycles

Bull and Bear Market Action

On any given day there is about a 70% likelihood that the stock market will move up and about a 30% likelihood it will go down. If you analyze long-term charts, the market looks like a series of steps – two or three forward, one or two back, but always eventually increasing over time. Corrections of 5%, 10%, and 15% of any given advance are commonplace. No so common are full-fledged bear markets that are so called when any market decline exceeds 20% or more. Bear market declines are usually very swift and rarely announce their arrival and yet they occur with a fair degree of regularity. In fact we've had many more bear markets during the last century, which implies we've experienced just as many bull markets as well. Bull markets follows bear, follows bull, follows bear, follows bull – it has always been thus.

Bull markets thrive on a robust economy, with low interest rates and easy money, low inflation, fuller employment, undervalued stocks with low price earnings multiples and higher dividend yields. Bull markets always begin in the depths of depression when most people are disillusioned from the previous bear market decline and the typical mindset is one of pessimism, fear, and disbelief. As the new bull market begins over time, a new mindset develops based on optimism and eventually greed replaces the fear however the market will climb a wall of worry all the way to the top.

The average decline lasts about one year and the average advance lasts four or more years. As well the average advance of 75% to 100% outpaces the average decline of 30% to 35% by a ratio of 3 to 1 times.

Bull/Bear Market Cycle

Market cycles move through four distinct quadrants to complete each cycle beginning with a bottom accumulation phase that often extends into an advanced bull phase lasting two or more years. Eventually, the market enters a correction phase and at the point that the market corrects 20% from its previous peak it officially becomes a bear market.

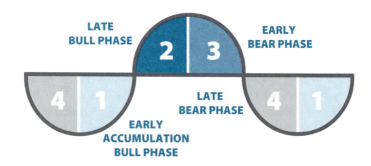

Typical Investment Cycle

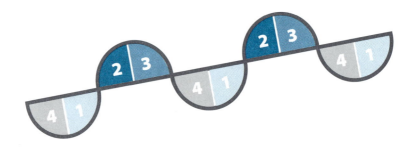

Market cycles are always based on a series of extremes influenced by investors fear and greed. The greatest risk is trying to time the market.

Typically each bull/bear cycle moves through the four quadrants with each one performing a little better than its previous cycle. Some cycles are more severe and prolonged such as the 1929–1932 Depression era in the US or the lost decades experienced by Japan in the 1990s and 2000s, which has witnessed a series of bear market rallies (dead cat bounces) only to experience a series of bear cycles reaching new market lows.

NIKKEI 225 Index

From 1966 to 1990 the Nikkei 225 Index in Japan grew from 1,000 to a whopping 39,000, a 3800% increase; during that same 25-year span the Dow Jones Industrial Average in the US grew from 1,000 to 3,000. The Japanese market outperformed the US by a ratio of 19 to 1.

The Nikkei 225 Index peaked at about 39,000 in 1989 then declined 50% in 3 years. For the next 17 years, it grinded lower in a declining "L" formation. The Japanese economy has been influenced by demographic factors: they have a seriously aging population and virtually zero immigration.

Bull markets always begin in the depth of depression when most people are disillusioned from the previous bear market decline and the typical mindset is one of pessimism, fear and disbelief.

Did You Know?

Japan's Nikkei 225 Index

From 1990 to 2009 Japan's Nikkei 225 Index rallied more than 30% 10 times and on four of those occasions the Nikkei soared over 50%. And yet the Nikkei still sits 50% lower than where the first of these 10 rallies began almost two decades ago.

Consider This!

Business Cycles

The world economy is in constant motion. Business activity expands and contracts through the cycles. Over time each cycle usually surpasses its previous high point. Investors must condition themselves to avoid the "noise of the markets" such as slowdown, recession, tariffs, trade deficits, currency devaluation, soft or hard landings, over or under priced, inflation, capital spending, etc. Just know that bull markets follow bear markets – it's the formula for free enterprise. Your success to a great extent will be based on how you handle your emotions throughout the cycles. Ignore the "noise of the markets" and maintain and manage the stewardship of your investments through every cycle. You will be well rewarded over time.

Markets are constantly in a state of uncertainty and flux and money is made by discounting the obvious and betting on the unexpected.

– George Soros

The Efficient Frontier

The efficient frontier of portfolio management theory advocates that there is an optimal level of diversification for every investor where the overall risk is minimized and the potential returns are maximized.

By investing in all possible combinations of stocks and bonds, from a 100% bond portfolio to a 100% stock portfolio, the efficient frontier illustrates how just a small allocation to stocks can actually reduce risk and increase your return. Using historical data for Canadian markets over the past half century a 100% bond portfolio yielded a 7.4% return; whereas a 80% bond/20% stock portfolio returned 8%; a better return and with less risk.

Historically, domestic economic cycles and foreign stock market cycles did not move in tandem over the long term therefore global investing provided some counterbalance to a Canadian bond and stock portfolio. This optimal level on the efficient frontier can be achieved with between 40% to 50% foreign content.

Efficient Frontier – Canadian Securities

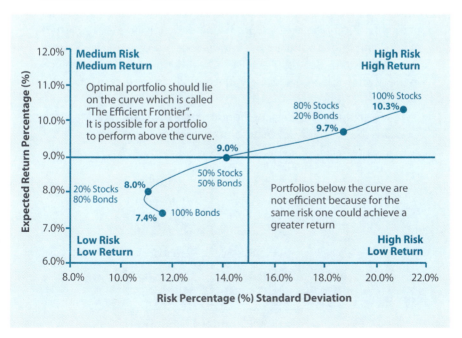

Risk versus Return

Professional pension fund managers embrace the concept of Modern Portfolio Theory, which includes the idea of investing on the Efficient Frontier (see diagram). It is a curve that represents the optimal return for each level of risk. Asset classes near the bottom left have low risk and low returns whereas asset classes near the upper right offer higher returns and higher risks.

Traditionally, DB pension fund managers allocate assets under management as follows:

Reserves   3% – 7%
Fixed Income   30% – 40%
Equities   55% – 65%

The efficient frontier of portfolio management theory advocates that there is an optimal level of diversification for every investor where the overall risk is minimized and the potential returns are maximized.

The teaching principle that members in DC plans can learn from this strategy is to emulate similar Modern Portfolio Theory in the allocation of their pension plan assets. Once your initial allocation is established in line with your comfort zone with respect to risk, you need only ensure that your portfolio remains efficient, throughout the swings in the economy by rebalancing your portfolio from time to time.

If we were to plot The Efficient Frontier curve on a graph divided into quartiles the various risk versus return scenarios are as follows:

Did You Know?

Mathematically, the Efficient Frontier is the intersection of the Set of Portfolios with Minimum Variance and the Set of Portfolios with Maximum Return.

Consider This!

There is no time for FEAR in a bear market. Successful investors embrace the following traits: FAITH, ENTHUSIASM, AMBITION, and RESOURCEFULLNESS.

You get recessions, you have stock market declines. If you don't understand that's going to happen, then you're not ready. You won't do well in the markets.

– Peter Lynch

SECTION 6
RETIREMENT WELLNESS

How Much Money Will You Need to Retire?

What does financial independence mean to you? In a financial context independence for most people is often defined as the freedom to choose when to retire from the workplace, on your terms and feeling assured that you'll have enough income to look after you and your loved ones, comfortably, for the rest of your lifetime.

How much money do you think **ME, Inc.** might need to save in order to be financially comfortable at retirement? Depending on whom you talk to, this figure ranges from $500,000 to $1,500,000 for the vast majority of Canadians. In fact, when government was designing the income security programs for Canadians (see table below) they felt that typically retirees would be comfortable if they could replace two thirds of their employment income based on the average national wage. And many advisors in the financial services industry recommend trying to achieve a 70% to 80% income replacement ratio while some mutual fund companies suggest you'll need to replace 85% to 90% or more of your pre-retirement income.

Canadian Income Replacement Ratios

While the income replacement ratios recommended above are ideal, the reality is that most people's retirement income is substantially less, often in the 40% to 60% range and they still live quite comfortably. Of course, it's in the best interests of the government and the financial services media to encourage Canadians to strive for much higher levels of savings and investing during the accumulation phase of one's life. However, the suggestion that you may suffer a life of hardship and even poverty if you don't save enough – is simply not true.

In 2010, the average national wage in Canada was $47,200 per annum. Many Canadians approaching retirement enjoy a pre-retirement income between $45,000 and $70,000 per year. As you can see on the following chart their post-retirement income averages between $27,000 and $31,500, which equates to an income replacement ratio of 45% to 60%. And according to Statistics Canada, only one in six Canadians with a pre-retirement income of $40,000 or more has an income replacement ratio of 75% or more. If you are one of the 36% of Canadian employees who is privileged to enjoy the benefits of an employer-sponsored pension or savings plan during your career you are truly blessed.

Income Replacement Ratios

Pre-Retirement Income	Post-Retirement Income	Actual Replacement Ratio
$70,000	$31,500	45%
$45,000	$27,000	60%
$10,000	$15,000	150%

The $500,000 ME, Inc. Retirement Dream

Ideally, by age 65, everyone should have a minimum liquid or "spendable" estate worth at least $500,000 over and above their pension incomes and fixed assets such as housing or accommodation (see table).

We assume money, in this example, is compounding at 6% annually. To acquire $500,000, starting at age 25, it would take $251 per month or a lump sum investment of $45,631. If you waited just 10 years to age 35, it would take $498 per month or a lump sum of $83,021 to reach $500,000. Delaying your investment program for 10 years has forced the monthly ante up by two times.

Now look what happens if you wait until age 45. The cost soars from $251 a month at age 25 to $1,082 or a 431% increase! Finally, if you're like many people who put off retirement planning, or even thinking about retirement until you are age 55 or older, it takes $3,051 per month or a $274,816 lump sum to accomplish that same $500,000 goal. Start retirement saving yesterday! Now you know why.

$500,000 Retirement Dream

Age	Monthly Contribution	or	Lump Sum Contribution	Years of Compounding	Rate of Return	Retirement Dream
25	$251		$45,631	40	6%	$500,000
35	$498		$83,021	30	6%	$500,000
45	$1,082		$151,048	20	6%	$500,000
55	$3,051		$274,816	10	6%	$500,000

Your Retirement Mortgage

Create the mindset to establish a retirement mortgage of $500,000. Say you plan to retire in 30 years then you will need to invest $498 per month at 6% to achieve your $500,000 goal. The key to your success is to think of this plan as an obligation that requires monthly deposits just like a mortgage.

$1,500,000 Retirement Dream

Age	Monthly Contribution	or	Lump Sum Contribution	Years of Compounding	Rate of Return	Retirement Dream
25	$753		$136,893	40	6%	$1,500,000
35	$1,493		$249,063	30	6%	$1,500,000
45	$3,246		$453,144	20	6%	$1,500,000
55	$9,153		$824,449	10	6%	$1,500,000

The Three-legged Resources Stool

Canadian seniors have three potential sources of income at retirement often referred to as a three-legged resources stool, which is a simple and marvelous time-tested design that consists of:

1. Government pension plans
2. Employer-sponsored arrangements
3. Personal savings.

For many Canadians, the question of how much they'll need to save for retirement will be dependent on whether they have a two-legged or a three-legged income resources stool at retirement.

Those individuals who are fortunate to have the benefit of employer-sponsored plans compounding in the background during their working careers, often discover that this leg provides the major source of their income at retirement. And those employees who have not had an employer-sponsored plan most often discover a significant financial shortfall at retirement unless they have maintained a disciplined personal savings and investment program — most have simply not saved nearly enough!

If you are one of the 36% of Canadian employees who is privileged to enjoy the benefits of an employer-sponsored registered pension plan (RPP) or savings plan during your career you are truly blessed.

Government income security programs – Old Age Security (OAS), a universal plan based on residency and the Canada/Québec Pension Plan (CPP/QPP), a contributory plan based on work income – are the first leg of the three-legged stool. Government plans are designed to replace 40% of the wages of an average worker's pre-retirement income. Individuals entitled to the maximum would receive in excess of $17,000 income annually from these programs. Those individuals who do not qualify for the full amount of these benefits and assuming they have little or no income from the other two legs of the stool can apply for further means-tested government assistance from the Guaranteed Income Supplement (GIS) plan.

Case Profile: Brad and Simone — in Their Late Fifties

Brad and Simone are married with three adult children. Brad has worked for a large utility company for the past 32 years and has an income of $90,000; Simone focused on the children and was a homemaker spouse for 13 years but prior to that had worked as an administrative assistant at a textile company for 12 years. She went back to the textile industry on a part-time basis six years ago.

Brad has been a member of his employers-sponsored pension plan throughout his career. His company offers a defined contribution (DC) pension plan that enables Brad to contribute up to 10% of his employment income and the company matches 75% on his contributions up to 6%, which equates to a 4 ½% maximum company contribution. Brad is planning to work for five more years at which point he will have 37 years of service and he anticipates he will have accumulated a retirement account balance of $575,000 at his retirement date.

Brad expects the next five years will unfold as follows: their home currently valued at $425,000 will be mortgage free; their adult children's education needs will be completed and he and Simone will be empty nesters. Simone anticipates her income will average about $25,000 per year for the next five years by which time Brad believes that he and Simone will have accumulated an additional $150,000 in RRSP and TFSA assets.

At retirement, Brad and Simone expect to generate $28,000 income per year from government resources; $34,500 annually from Brad's company pension plan based on $575,000 retirement balance invested at 6% and $10,500 income per year from the RRSP/TFSA assets. If all goes according to plan Brad and Simone will have a total retirement income of $73,000 which works out to an income replacement ratio of 63% based on their combined net annual salaries.

Income Replacement Ratio
Net Annual Pensions $73,000
Brad and Simone's Net Annual Salaries $115,000 x 100% = 63%

In summary, Brad and Simone have the support of a three-legged stool, which is a simple and marvelous time-tested design. With three sturdy legs, it will provide them with strong and stable support in their retirement years.

Pre-retirees measure their retirement income expectations three ways: monthly, annual, and lump sum income.

- The majority, 60% viewed their retirement income as a monthly income stream (average amount $4,000)
- About 30% measured their retirement income as an annual income stream (average amount $60,000)
- A few, 10% measured their retirement income based on a lump sum (average amount $750,000)

These figures are based on our seminar surveys at the Institute. Note that all of the seminar respondents have employer-sponsored pension arrangements.

Consider This!

The three essential ingredients of retirement success based on employer sponsored pension or savings arrangements are contributions, returns, and time.

- **Contributions** – the amount of money that was invested
- **Returns** – the average net rate of return
- **Time** – the length of time the money stayed invested

These three factors combined result in satisfaction or disappointment at retirement. To get more out of a Capital Accumulation Plan (CAP), there are only three things you can do:

- Increase the amount going in (and make no withdrawals before retirement)
- Increase the rate of return (invest to your maximum level of risk with a low-cost balanced, diversified portfolio)
- Increase the holding period (join early, retire later, use a registered retirement income fund or life income fund to stretch the holding period).

Three Sources of Income
1. Person at work
2. Money at work
3. Charity (welfare)

Man's mind, once stretched by a new idea, never regains its original shape.
– **Oliver Wendell Holmes**

Freedom 55 – Myth or Reality?

How soon before you reach the distribution phase of your life? When do you expect to retire? How long will you live in retirement? Will your current asset allocation strategies meet your needs for a retirement that could last 30 years or longer? These are the kind of questions you need to consider when you are on the doorstep of retirement. In recent surveys conducted by the Institute the following statistics for Canadians were revealed:

- 36% have a company-sponsored registered pension plan
- 45% feel they are not saving enough for retirement
- 57% expect to work at least part time during retirement
- 60% do not have a written financial and life planning blueprint.

The notion of retiring as early as age 55 is nothing more than a pipe dream for most people. With the onslaught of 2008–09 Great Recession and its severity, many Canadians now envision having to work into their late 60s or early 70s.

The New Retirement Reality
Retirement is no longer a single event; for many individuals it is an evolutionary transition from full-time work to complete retirement through a series of phased steps that may last over a period of a few years to a few decades. Our latest surveys at the Institute indicate that 28% of Canadians would like to continue to work full time for an additional 2 to 3 years beyond the normal retirement age of 65; and another 2 to 3 years on a part time basis into their early 70s.

Each individual's retirement transition will evolve differently: some will stay at their current place of work; some will work reduced daily hours while others will compress the work week down to 1 or 2 days; and some will move to a new employer or to a different line of work that they feel more passionate about.

Reasons for a Phased Retirement
Phased retirement is a process of exploration that involves lifestyle considerations and change. It is a time to review, recreate, redefine, rejuvenate, reevaluate, reinvent, re-hire, or as my IT friends would say, "a time to reboot!"

Many reasons are given for phased retirements including:

- Fear of leaving security of workplace
- Financially unprepared for full retirement
- Fear of outliving capital
- Want to continue being active
- Want to explore less stressful work opportunities
- Want to increase standard of living
- Want to maintain a continuing sense of purpose
- Health concerns
- Want to maintain identity and self-esteem
- Want to explore new work opportunities

Retirement is no longer a single event; for many individuals it is an evolutionary transition from full-time work to complete retirement through a series of phased steps that may last over a period of a few years to a few decades.

There are numerous ways to fulfill the task of working in retirement, which would include the following work options: full time, part time, job sharing, work sharing, multi-tracking, and talent pooling. As well, you'll need to decide whether you want to work as an employee or would you rather be self-employed as an entrepreneur, agent, contractor, or consultant.

Did You Know?

Lee Iacocca, President of the Ford Motor Division left after having amassed a multi-million dollar net worth. After a few short months in retirement including extensive vacation travel, Iacocca found nothing in retirement as fulfilling as his work used to be. His strong work ethic, his sense of purpose, and his unbridled ambition led him back to work in the auto industry at Chrysler.

One in four older workers (age 55 to 64) are self-employed and one in five work part time.

– Statistics Canada

The Two-Legged Resources Stool

What if you have the support of only a two-legged stool at retirement? We have learned that about two thirds of Canadian workers do not have an employer-sponsored registered pension plan. So how should they prepare for a secure retirement? Quite simply, they have to place much more emphasis on the personal resources leg of the stool in order to achieve a reasonable degree of financial security for their retirement. Let's take a look at how a self-employed couple approached their retirement.

Case Profile: Frank and Alicia Garcia and – in Their Early Sixties
Frank and Alicia met, while they were both working in the printing industry 30 years ago. They decided to make printing their career and with the help of other family members they opened their own print shop. Frank worked at the business full time and Alicia worked at the business part time, while raising their two children. The Garcia's own their own home outright and have recently become empty nesters. They have drawn a combined income of $90,000 most years and after allowing for all household and family expenses they have made limited RRSP contributions, which are currently valued at $260,000.

In a recent discussion with the account manager at their bank it was suggested that they should target 70% income replacement at retirement. After the meeting Frank started to do some cursory planning regarding their financial status and wondered if they could retire in two to three years. Frank discovered that he will be entitled to maximum government benefits from OAS and CPP and Alicia will receive maximum OAS and partial CPP estimated at 70% from these two programs.

Two thirds of Canadian workers do not have an employer-sponsored registered pension plan.

Government Income Security Programs
Maximum Payments – 2010

Person	Resource	Amount
Frank	OAS	$6,259
	CPP	$11,210
Alicia	OAS	$6,259
	CPP	$7,634
Total Annual Income from Government Resources		**$31,362**

Frank and Alicia will receive about $31,000 per year from government plans. Assuming they owned their own home and the mortgage was paid off, their children's education needs were completed and they were now empty nesters, and they no longer had expenses pertaining to the workplace, they might find that they could live quite comfortably on 40% to 50% of their pre-work income in retirement.

However, based on the suggested target of a 70% income replacement ratio in retirement as suggested by their banker the Garcia's would need (70% x $90,000 annual income = $63,000). With only $31,362 provided by government plans the balance ($63,000-$31,362 = $31,638) will have to be provided from their RRSPs and personal investments.

The amount of investment capital needed to generate the additional income desired of $31,638 at various rates of return are in the following table:

Rate of Return Required to Fund Retirement Income	Retirement Capital Required to Earn $31,638
4%	$790,950
5%	$632,760
6%	$527,300
7%	$451,971
8%	$395,475

With *RRSPs worth $260,000 the Garcias are facing a capital shortfall to fund their retirement. Even a conservative return of 6% will require retirement capital of $527,300 to meet their goal of a 70% income replacement ratio. Therefore, the Garcias have the following choices:*

- **Retire at a Lower Standard of Living than Planned** – *By accepting a less costly lifestyle of a 50% to 55% replacement ratio, the Garcias will be able to retire as planned. They are not alone; in fact the average replacement ratio for Canadians at their income level is 45% even though the dream is to retire at a loftier level of 70% to 80%. Should the markets perform well during the next few years and/or if their $260,000 RRSP assets returned greater than a 6% return they still end up with a fair degree of comfort in their retirement.*

- **Remain in the Work Force Longer** – *The Garcias could maintain their working careers for a few extra years so that they can accumulate more capital. Frank figures they could accumulate an additional $150,000 if they delayed their retirement by five years and at a 6% return would provide an additional $9,000 income per year.*

- **Change the Targeted Rate of Growth on Their Portfolios** – *By attempting to obtain higher rates of return by increasing the equity exposure in their accounts, the Garcias might be able to achieve their desired 70% replacement ratio. However, they are simply not willing to roll the dice at this stage of the life cycle. What if taking the extra risk backfired? The question every investor needs to ask prior to investing in the equity markets is, "What is your sleep factor?" The sleepless nights and added stress if markets went into a negative cycle are just not worth it.*

Did You Know?

Canadian Pension Statistics

- 71% of family units or 9.4 million have pension assets.
- 58% of family units have RRSPs, RRIFs, and LIRAs with median value of $30,000.
- 49% of family units have employer RPPs with median value of $68,300.
- 69.4% of Canadians aged 55 – 64 have RRSPs with median value of $60,000 and average values of $124,500. This includes employer pension plan conversions to locked-in plans.

– Statistics Canada, July 2008

Consider This!

How Much Have American Workers Saved for Retirement?

Savings	All Workers	Aged 55+
Less than $10,000	40%	30%
$10,001 – $50,000	24%	19%
$50,001 – $100,000	12%	10%
$100,001 – $250,000	12%	15%
$250,000 or more	12%	26%

Note that 64% of all workers report that the total value of their household's savings and investments excluding the value of their primary home and defined benefit pension plans is less than $50,000; and 20% say they have less than $1,000 in savings.

– Retirement Confidence Survey, 2009, Employee Benefit Research Institute

Section 6 Retirement Wellness

Living Expenses Decrease in Retirement

Have you ever given serious thought to what your expenses will be in retirement? Many studies suggest that most individuals' expenses will decrease by 30% to 40% or more at retirement. In the previous module we discussed how much money you would need in retirement and what a realistic range of income replacement ratios might be. Now it's time to take a look at the flow of your income in retirement.

The notion that you'll need a set percentage of your pre-retirement income each year throughout your retirement is not realistic. There are four possible directions that each of your expenses for **ME, Inc**. might take in retirement: some will vanish completely, others will decrease, some may increase, and others will not change at all.

The reality for most people is that they will spend more on leisure and lifestyle expenses in the early years of retirement and less in the later years; and substantially more on health related expenses in the later years as depicted in the graph below.

Retirement Living Expenses

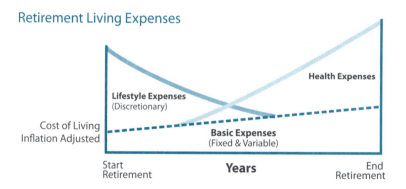

In the case profile for Shan Chen we'll take a look at how she projects her retirement expenses allocations.

Case Profile: Shan Chen, age 62, Projected Retirement Expenses
Shan has worked as an administrator for an Ontario college for the past 33 years and currently earns $64,000 annually. She is fortunate to have had the opportunity to participate in her employer's defined benefit pension plan and she anticipates that this resource will provide the majority of her income at retirement.

Shan expects to have an annual income of $45,000 in retirement made up of a $24,000 employer pension, $16,000 of government pensions, and $5,000 of personal resources.

At retirement, Shan's expenses will decrease substantially. She will no longer pay into Canada Pension Plan or Employment Insurance, and her employer pension plan contributions will cease. The many years of saving in preparation for retirement will now be behind her. Work-related expenses (transportation, clothing, and meals) will vanish. When her daughter's education needs are fulfilled and she leaves home, this expense will disappear as well.

Shan's income taxes in retirement will decrease as will the costs of running her home now that the mortgage is paid off. Her transportation costs will decline as she will no longer need to drive her car to work. Shan believes her expenses for food, recreation, reading, and education will remain about the same. However, she anticipates that travel, leisure activities, health and personal care expenses will all cost more.

There are four possible directions that each of your expenses for ME, Inc. might take in retirement: some will vanish completely, others will decrease, some may increase, and others will not change at all.

Living Expenses in Retirement

Major Components	O Vanish	< Decrease	= No Change	> Increase
CPP/EI Deductions	✔			
Employer Pension Plan Contributions	✔			
Children's Education	✔			
Child Care – Empty Nest	✔			
Work Expenses – Transportation, Clothing, Meals	✔			
Saving for Retirement	✔			
Income Taxes		✔		
Transportation		✔		
Food			✔	
Recreation, Reading, and Education			✔	
Health and Personal Care				✔
Travel				✔
Leisure Activities				✔
Mortgage / Rent		✔		
Other:				
Other:				

Did You Know?

Net worth is the most important variable in determining an individual's expectations for retirement spending as well as the most important determinant of a retiree's actual spending. Higher net worth retirees spend more than lower net worth retirees.

Consider This!

Our lives don't always turn out the way we planned — there can be many turning points such as a separation/divorce, disability, serious illness, downsize/early leave, or major financial loss to mention a few. And each of these life events can derail the best-laid plans. In the words of John Lennon, "Life is what happens to you while you're busy making other plans." Many individuals will not be able to retire as planned — some will need to work. If that becomes your destiny, try to select work that you are passionate about, that is fulfilling and provides you with a sense of purpose.

The less money you need to fund your consumption during your working years, the more you can save for retirement. And the lower your inherent lifestyle expenses now, the less money you'll need to maintain your lifestyle in retirement.

You can be young without money but you can't be old without it.
— Tennessee Williams

The key to a happy retirement is to have enough money to live on, but not enough to worry about.
— Unknown

As in all successful ventures, the foundation of a good retirement is planning.
— Earl Nightingale

Section 6 Retirement Wellness

How to Determine Your Retirement Age Goal

Sooner or later every working Canadian wrestles with the questions, "At what age should I retire and have I got enough money to go?" Your retirement age goal will depend upon lifecycle events such as: when your working career began, when you bought your home, at what age you began your family, to mention a few. For example, if you leave your job at age 57 with 28 years of service in your employer pension plan your retirement income might be $24,000 per year versus leaving at age 62 with 33 years of service and a retirement income of $30,000 per year. The additional five years of service in this example increased the final pension payout by $6,000 per year, which is a 25% increase over the pension amount that would be received by retiring five years sooner.

There is a substantial difference in income at retirement if you leave early because you have:

- Five years less pension accumulation growth
- Five years less pension contributions
- Five years more pension withdrawals
- Five more years to be concerned about maintaining your purchasing power.

Retirement Age Goal

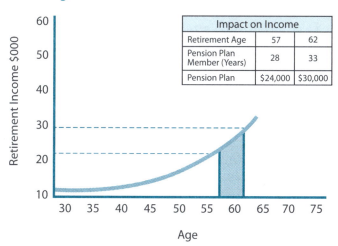

Impact on Income		
Retirement Age	57	62
Pension Plan Member (Years)	28	33
Pension Plan	$24,000	$30,000

Planning Your Retirement Income

At retirement, there are a number of planning initiatives for **ME, Inc.** to consider, to ensure you will have adequate income from your retirement resources. In fact, there are four major stages to consider when plotting your retirement income whereby you'll have the opportunity to structure your income stream as you age:

- **Stage One –** retirement from the workforce with a company pension. Generally, most corporate pension plans are structured with normal retirement at age 65, and early retirement at age 55.
- **Stage Two –** Canada Pension Plan/Québec Pension Plan (CPP/QPP) is available at age 65, however it can be taken as early as age 60 or as late as age 70 subject to an income adjustment. Old Age Security (OAS) commences at age 65.
- **Stage Three –** Convert RRSP to RRIF and or annuity no later than the end of the year you attain age 71. Should you have an income shortfall between your retirement date and the year in which you convert your RRSPs it is best to obtain funds from your non-registered investments. Note, in most cases this drawdown sequence through the first three stages will deliver tax efficiency while ensuring the longevity of your funds.
- **Stage Four –** Continue to work full time or part time ideally in a vocation that you are absolutely passionate about. When you work at something you really care about, it rarely feels like work.

By structuring the start date of your various income streams in retirement you give yourself a raise each time and by so doing provide yourself with an opportunity to offset inflation.

Case Profile: Walter Stevens, age 58, Projected Retirement Income
In the following chart you can track Walter's retirement income resources as he structures his income stream to suit his needs at each stage of the retirement cycle:

- *Walter retires at age 58 with $28,000 of annual pension income from a joint life annuity purchased from funds accumulated in his employers defined contribution (DC) retirement account balance.*
- *Two years later, Walter exercises his option to begin receiving reduced CPP benefits of $7,847 at age 60 instead of waiting until age 65. Income at age 60: $28,000 + $7,847 = $35,847.*

- OAS benefits will begin at age 65 which will add an additional $6,259 to his income. Income at age 65: $28,000 + $7,847 + $6,259 = $42,106.
- At age 71 Walter plans to convert his $180,000 RRSP into a RRIF. He has a solid base of fixed income from his employer's pension and his government benefits so he plans to allocate his RRIF 40% fixed income and 60% equities. Walter believes he can achieve a blended return of about 8% or $14,400. Income at age 71: $28,000 + $7,847 + $6,259 + $14,400 = $56,506.
- Walter's retirement income resources more than doubled in the 13 years from age 58 to 71.

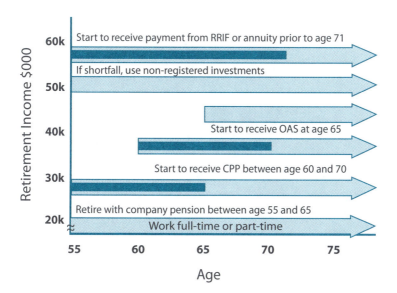

Did You Know?

People retiring today have the potential to live almost as long in retirement as they've spent saving for it. Most retirees do not want to take on too much volatility or risk. However, they need to understand that holding a portion of their assets in growth-oriented investments is necessary to achieve the returns that are going to last them through two or three decades of retirement.

Consider This!

Retirement is as much about time management as it is about money management.

Many people who leave the workforce in their early 50s find themselves looking for a new job within three months. They find out the greener grass called "Freedom 55" is not quite as attractive as they thought it would be. And with life expectancy increasing into the early 80s, and longer, the absence of work leaves many retirees feeling a loss of purpose.

I have enough money to last me the rest of my life, unless I buy something.

– Jackie Mason

If you don't want to work (in retirement), you have to work to earn enough money so that you won't have to work.

– Ogden Nash

Retirement: It's nice to get out of the rat race, but you have to learn to get along with less cheese.

– Gene Perret

What is a Sustainable Withdrawal Rate?

Perhaps the most difficult question for a retiree is "How much can I safely withdraw per year from my retirement assets?" Miscalculating could lead to one of two extremes: an involuntary return to the workforce or the problem of distributing a large net worth in your estate.

Myths and Realities
There are a number of myths associated with how an investor should go about calculating a sustainable withdrawal rate.

Myth
An investor can equate a sustainable annual withdrawal rate with a portfolio's expected long-term compound annual return.

The Reality
Portfolio volatility and the sequence in which returns occur will ultimately determine if a portfolio withdrawal rate is sustainable (defined as capital preservation in the face of annual withdrawals).

Myth
An investor can equate a sustainable annual withdrawal rate based on anticipated life expectancy rates.

The Reality
Average life expectancy rates point to the age at which 50% of the population will still be living. If withdrawal rates were based on this data many retirees would outlive their assets.

Myth
At retirement conventional wisdom suggests investors should sell equities and switch to bonds for the surety of long-term realistic sustainable income.

The Reality
For investors with more than 25 to 30 years and longer payout periods, portfolios with more than 30% bonds have more volatility, and lower total returns than more equity heavy asset allocations.

Studies show you could actually increase your chances of going broke by selling stocks and buying bonds.

The Bengen Study

William Bengen, a financial planner, looked at year-by-year returns from 1926–1994 for a retirement portfolio with 50% equities / 50% long-term bonds.

This asset allocation was able to sustain a 4.1% inflation adjusted withdrawal rate for any possible 30-year period since 1926.

Bengen concluded that a typical retirement fund with a 50/50 equity/fixed income mix allocation would enable a portfolio to survive the worst bear market declines. Note: this study included the Great Depression era of the 1930s.

What is an Inflation Adjusted Withdrawal Rate?

When you begin retirement the first step for **ME, Inc**. is to determine a "safe" withdrawal rate. This is generally calculated based on your anticipated life expectancy plus five or ten years (depending on your conservatism).

The second step is to determine the highest withdrawal rate that satisfies the desired minimum portfolio life based on a 50%/50% stock/bond allocation. For an investor aged 60 to 65 this would generally be about 4%.

The third step is to calculate the withdrawal amount for the first year based on a percentage times the starting value of the portfolio.

The final step requires an adjustment up or down for inflation every succeeding year based on the previous year's withdrawal.

Case Profile: Ingrid Johansen, Age 60, Ontario Resident

Ingrid retires at age 60 with a $400,000 accumulated retirement account balance in her employer-sponsored DC pension plan. She decides to convert her pension assets into a self-directed Life Income Fund (LIF). Based on the Bengen study she expects she can safely withdraw 4.1% inflation adjusted as follows:

Starting Retirement Account Balance	$400,000
1st Year – remove 4.1% of starting balance	($16,400)
Inflation during 1st year is 2.1%	($344)
2nd Year withdrawal	$16,744
Inflation during 2nd year is 3.4%	($569)
3rd Year withdrawal	$17,313

Note: LIFs, LRIFs, and RRIFs all have the same minimum withdrawal requirements. However, they differ on the maximum withdrawals: LIF and LRIF withdrawals are set by the jurisdiction that governs the plan e.g., the province or federal government, whereas RRIFs do not have a maximum. Did you know that all plans also permit another maturity option – the purchase of an insured life annuity?

The Harvard Study
Harvard analysts conducted a study in 1973 to measure a sustainable withdrawal rate from their endowment fund without eroding the principal.

Assuming a portfolio with 50% equity / 50% bonds they discovered a 4% inflation adjusted withdrawal rate was sustainable.

Trinity University Study
Researchers measured the success rate of various portfolios from 1926 to 1995 to calculate safe withdrawal rates.

They discovered an optimal mix of 75% equity / 25% long-term bonds would deliver an inflation adjusted return of 4% over 30 years with a 98% success rate.

Trinity concluded:
- Low safe withdrawal rates cause a suboptimal exchange of present consumption for future consumption and therefore a good chance of accumulating a large net worth.
- Portfolios with at least 75% equities can provide 4% to 5% inflation adjusted sustainable withdrawals over the long term.
- For shorter payout periods (15 years or less) withdrawal rates of 8% to 9% are sustainable.

Source: Retirement Savings: Choosing a Withdrawal Rate that is Sustainable by Philip L. Cooley, Carl M. Hubbard, Daniel T. Walz (professors of finance at Trinity University, San Antonio, TX)

Retirement Danger Zone
- Weak returns can sabotage a portfolio's lifespan
- Early year losses can erode the duration of the payout period

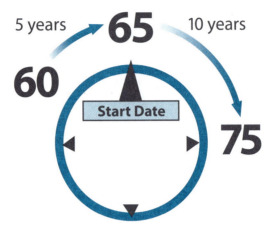

Section 6 Retirement Wellness

Did You Know?

Greatest Financial Security Risks

- The greatest financial security risk is the first five years after one's retirement start date.

- High withdrawal rates and poor market performance can decimate portfolio returns and significantly deplete one's capital.

- Volatility of returns is the clear and present danger that a retiree could suffer a permanent loss of living standards.

Consider This!

Build Safety Measures into Withdrawal Rates

- Start with as low a rate as possible;
- Adjust for inflation (index to CPI)

Setting the bar lower initially leaves room for growth of assets and a margin of safety to withstand portfolio volatility. Generally as retirees age they can increase withdrawal rates and decrease equity exposure.

As I tell anybody under age 50, you shouldn't be giving up hope. There's almost always some combination of living frugally and saving and investing wisely that can give you a viable retirement income as long as you've got 15 years to work on it.

– Malcolm Hamilton

SECTION 7
AFTERWORD

Putting Your Blueprint into Action!

Steps to Get Started

Congratulations! You have finished reading **ME, Inc.** and now it is time to put the knowledge you have acquired to practical use by commencing actionable applications with your financial blueprint. Let's take a look at a series of steps you can complete beginning today:

1. Make an honest assessment of your finances today by looking at a snapshot in time of your current Net Worth and Cash Flow statements for **ME, Inc.**

2. Review the Investment Personality Questionnaire for **ME, Inc**. to determine your comfort zone with respect to risk tolerance.

3. Know clearly what your investment timeframe is and with this knowledge you can determine your asset allocation mix. Remember that 90% of the variation in returns will be based on the asset allocation formula you choose for yourself.

4. Your company-sponsored pension plan is a long-term commitment, (other than for employees on the doorstep of retirement). You cannot access your pension assets until you retire and therefore your asset class selections should reflect your long-term investment timeframe. Build your pension portfolio from the selection of funds offered by your employer plan (if applicable).

5. Your asset class selections for your non-registered and personal investments should be based on the timeframe of your needs and goals (short, medium, or long-term), e.g. the purchase of a new car in one year would require a short-term investment timeframe. Use index funds if you are unsure which stocks or mutual funds to choose on your own. This is to ensure that your money is invested while you're waiting to figure out how to manage your portfolio for the longer term.

6. Consider establishing a relationship with an investment advisor or other financial professional.

Additional Resources for You to Consider

You have increased your knowledge substantially by reading this book; now you may be wondering what other resources and knowledge tools are available for your consideration.

There are a myriad of possibilities for you to consider:

- Take financial planning courses at a community college in person or via correspondence.
- Use the Internet to access investment data, economic forecasts, market statistics, research and benchmarks.
- Read the financial section of one of the national newspapers and track the performance of a few selected stocks and/or mutual funds.
- Subscribe to specialty financial newsletters.
- Consider joining an investment club.
- Establish a relationship with a financial professional or gather enough expertise to become a do-it-yourself (DIY) investor.

Looking to the future, your investment results will be dictated by your efforts to acquire financial knowledge and investment wisdom from great investment role models such as John Templeton, Peter Lynch, Warren Buffett, and so many others who have travelled this road before us. The bottom line is that when you start to learn about investing and have conversations with colleagues and other students of the market like yourself, good things start to happen. You become like whom you associate yourself with – it's as simple as that!

Closing Thoughts
We trust you have been able to acquire several financial nuggets as a result of the time you have invested in developing your **ME, Inc.** life blueprint. While the predominant theme has been about financial planning topics, do not lose sight of the bigger picture of your life plan that embraces the Six Powers of Success that we discussed in the first lesson of this book.

We wish you lots of good health, happiness, longevity, and may all of your financial planning dreams and lifestyle pursuits come true, along with a balanced and fulfilling lifestyle. But if we had only one final wish that we could leave with you for your life journey, it would be for a handful of precious relationships. On that final day of reckoning, the real marker of your life will be based on the lives of others that you have touched by making a difference and having left the gift of a lasting legacy.

Did You Know?

Our grandparents' wisdom was to "save for a rainy day." As it turns out — they were absolutely right. The grandparents' children were caught unawares in the financial crisis with a belief that the good times would last forever. They are now scrambling to pay down debts and focusing on putting some pension assets together for retirement with a motto of, "saving until death do us part."

Work like you don't need the money, love like your heart has never been broken, and dance like no one is watching.

– Aurora Greenway

APPENDIX 1

Investment Tips

Buy good businesses that you understand and invest for the long term. Discipline yourself to buy quality companies and as long as they remain good companies continue to add to your positions.

Look for companies with a history of increasing sales and revenues: increasing earnings, and a history of paying out a substantial portion of the earnings with increasing dividends.

Diversify your portfolio by company, by industry, by country, by currency.

Portfolios should be rebalanced at regular intervals to maintain your asset class ratios in line with your risk tolerance profile and investment timeframe.

If an investment sounds too good to be true, it probably is.

Always use the economic law of supply and demand before you decide to invest. When supply is greater than the demand prices tend to go down and vice versa.

Look for businesses with a unique franchise where there is less likelihood of existing or new competition from rival businesses.

Review your investment objectives on a regular basis – at a minimum conduct an annual financial fire drill. However, beware of too much planning and very little execution.

That which is hardest to do is probably correct. If ever you find yourself hoping instead of believing, it is probably time to liquidate your position.

Invest for the long term in fundamentally sound companies. Don't be shortsighted – most investors focus on daily, weekly, and monthly results rather than quarterly, yearly, and longer-term growth scenarios.

Look for outstanding management with an established track record with a significant stake in the company. It is important that management share in the same risk/rewards as all other shareholders as they will be more apt to treat their fellow shareholders fairly.

The essence of a sound investment is the purchase of a substantial future earning power at the lowest price possible.

Invest 90% of the equity allocation of your portfolio in major well-seasoned proven companies with limited downside risk. Allocate 10% of your portfolio to other more junior and speculative investments where the risk reward is much greater. This will enable you to earn a better overall return without taking undue risk by endangering your overall capital position.

Investors must be able to read and digest financial statements, prospectuses, and other key research reports issued by a company in order to understand the fundamental and technical outlook, the motivation of its management, the competitive nature of its industry, and the perception of the company in its marketplace.

It is easier to make money in a declining (bear) market than in an advancing (bull) market because the downside risks are lower. One of the observations all investors eventually learn is that it is easier to lose money than to make money in the market, therefore, if one can minimize the downside risk you have won half the battle.

Cut your losses early by selling your losers and holding on to your winners. The first loss is most often the smallest loss and as time goes on, losses can multiply very quickly.

The best time to buy securities is when others are fearful and willing to sell at bargain basement prices and to sell securities when others are driven by greed and willing to purchase at astronomical prices.

When investing – the best offense is a good defense. So who, above all else can you trust – only yourself!

The media almost always will attempt to put a positive slant on the market and economy. Always remember that the media are self-serving to their owners and advertisers and are reporting stale news – yesterday's facts. However, the art of investing successfully is always about tomorrow's news.

The stock market is always more concerned with the future than the present. It is a leading indicator that generally anticipates the trend several months in advance.

The two major market drivers for investors are fear and greed and they are stronger than long-term resolve.

Long-term price earnings ratios for the past century average 15 times earnings. Generally stocks are perceived as representing good value when trading under 10 times earnings and less valuable or more expensive when trading above 20 times earnings.

Be mindful that the definition of real wealth means what's left after taxes, inflation, fees, costs, and management expenses.

Use dollar cost averaging and invest regularly to smooth out volatility – you buy more investment units when prices are low and fewer when they are high.

Consider the impact of taxes on your portfolio. The type of investment income you earn, as well as the type of account you hold your investments in can have tax implications. Your after-tax return on investments is of most importance.

APPENDIX 2

Best/Worst Days by Percent Change and Point Change DJIA 1901 to 2009 (March)

The following tables provide an incredible history of the markets best and worst days in percentage changes and point changes. A review of the 12 best days reveals that nine of the days occurred during the 1929 to 1933 corridor when the US was facing the Great Depression. Two of the best days took place during the Great Recession when the DJIA increased by 11.1% on October 13, 2008, and two weeks later it increased by another 10.9% on October 28, 2008. It is interesting to note that two of the worst trading days for the DJIA took place on October the 9th and 15th of 2008, declining 7.3% and 7.9%, respectively. Without a doubt, October 2008 was one of the most volatile periods ever in market history.

The absolute worst day ever experienced in the DJIA was a loss of 22.6% on October 19, 1987, when the market witnessed a period of climax selling that led to a waterfall correction of 36% over a period of two months. Two days later on October 21, 1987, the market rallied for a gain of 10.2% and this was followed by another decline of 8% on October 26, 1987.

You will note that six of the 12 worst days ever took place between 1929 and 1932 during The Great Depression and three of the worst days occurred in 2008 during the Great Recession.

Confidence did not dissolve overnight, rather through September and October while the market declined overall, there were many positive days along with the negative days and volume was extremely high throughout the period. Two of the dead cat bounces were substantial: plus 12.3% on October 30, 1929, and plus 9.4% on November 14, 1929.

BEST Days by Percent and Point
DJIA 1901 to 2009

By Percent Change				By Point Change			
Day	Close	PNT Change	% Change	Day	Close	PNT Change	% Change
03/15/33	62.10	8.26	15.3	10/30/29	258.47	28.40	12.3
10/06/31	99.34	12.86	14.9	11/14/29	217.28	18.59	9.4
10/30/29	258.47	28.40	12.3	10/05/29	341.36	16.19	5.0
09/21/32	75.16	7.67	11.4	10/31/29	273.51	15.04	5.8
10/13/08	9387.61	936.42	11.1	10/13/08	9387.61	936.42	11.1
10/28/08	9065.12	889.35	10.9	10/28/08	9065.12	889.35	10.9
10/21/87	2027.85	186.84	10.2	11/13/08	8835.25	552.59	6.7
08/03/32	58.22	5.06	9.5	10/06/31	99.34	12.86	14.9
02/11/32	78.60	6.80	9.5	11/15/29	228.73	11.45	5.3
11/14/29	217.28	18.59	9.4	06/19/30	228.97	10.13	4.6
12/18/31	80.69	6.90	9.4	09/05/39	148.12	10.03	7.3
02/13/32	85.82	7.22	9.2	11/22/28	290.34	9.81	3.5

WORST Days by Percent and Point
DJIA 1901 to 2009

By Percent Change				By Point Change			
Day	Close	PNT Change	% Change	Day	Close	PNT Change	% Change
10/19/87	1738.74	-508.00	-22.6	09/29/08	10365.45	-777.68	-7.0
10/28/29	260.64	-38.33	-12.8	10/28/29	260.64	-38.33	-12.8
10/29/29	230.07	-30.57	-11.7	10/29/29	230.07	-30.57	-11.7
11/06/29	232.13	-25.55	-9.9	11/06/29	232.13	-25.55	-9.9
08/12/32	63.11	-5.79	-8.4	10/23/29	305.85	-20.66	-6.3
03/14/07	55.84	-5.05	-8.3	11/11/29	220.39	-16.14	-6.8
10/26/87	1793.93	-156.83	-8.0	10/15/08	8577.91	-733.08	-7.9
10/15/08	8577.91	-733.08	-7.9	09/17/01	8920.70	-684.81	-7.1
07/21/33	88.71	-7.55	-7.8	11/04/29	257.68	-15.83	-5.8
10/18/37	125.73	-10.57	-7.8	12/12/29	243.14	-15.30	-5.9
12/01/08	8149.09	-679.95	-7.7	12/01/08	8149.09	-679.95	-7.7
10/09/08	8579.19	-678.91	-7.3	10/09/08	8579.13	-678.91	-7.3